OVERCOMING SCHOOL AVOIDANCE

OVERCOMING SCHOOL AVOIDANCE

WHAT TO DO WHEN YOUR KID WON'T GO TO SCHOOL

JAYNE DEMSKY

Founder of the School Avoidance Alliance

UNION SQUARE & CO. and the distinctive Union Square & Co. logo
are trademarks of Hachette Book Group, Inc.

This book is intended solely for adult readers, and is for informational purposes only. The publisher does not claim that it will provide or guarantee any benefits, healing, cure, or any other results. For medical advice, diagnosis, and treatment, it is necessary to consult with a physician or other licensed medical professional.

Any trademarks, names, logos, and designs are the property of their owners. Unless specifically identified as such, use herein of any third-party trademarks, company names, or celebrity or personal names, likenesses, images, or quotations, does not indicate any relationship, sponsorship, or endorsement between the author, the publisher, and the trademark owner, company, celebrity, or person.

ISBN 978-1-4549-5804-8 (paperback)
ISBN 978-1-4549-5805-5 (e-book)

Library of Congress Cataloging-in-Publication Data is available upon request.

Union Square & Co. books may be purchased in bulk for business, educational, or promotional use. For more information, please contact your local bookseller or the Hachette Book Group's Special Markets department at special.markets@hbgusa.com.

Printed in Canada

MRQ-T

1 2025

unionsquareandco.com

Cover design by Kaylie Pendleton
Cover art by Shutterstock.com: Margaret M Stewart (notebook)
Interior design by Christine Heun

For my son Matthew, and in loving memory and gratitude to my parents, Sandy and Lenny Rosen.

Contents

Introduction

Every Wednesday at around 6:00 p.m., I start counting down to a standing appointment that has been a part of my life for the past three years. By 7:10 p.m., I find the quietest room in my home, power up my laptop, take a deep breath, and prepare a few go-to topics to fill any potential silences. At 7:29 p.m., I open my Zoom link and watch as participants join the meeting. This is the School Avoidance Alliance Parent Peer-to-Peer Support Group.

Despite the varied causes, contributing factors, and manifestations of each child's school avoidance, common threads unite us as parents, humans, and determined advocates. Our group discussions revolve around the current challenges our families face and how we can support each other.

We exchange frustrating stories—one parent shares that their school district is sending their child to truancy court for school-avoidant absenteeism caused by anxiety, depression, and post-traumatic stress disorder (PTSD) from losing a father and brother in the same year. We celebrate victories, such as when a family finds an experienced therapist who collaborates on a plan using evidence-based strategies to help their child. And we rejoice in the stories that make me jump for joy, like when a child returns to school after weeks of absence and fully reintegrates.

At the end of each support group meeting, I feel encouraged, hopeful, and deeply appreciative of these families who are so dedicated to helping their children, as well as others who are facing similar challenges.

Forming the School Avoidance Alliance has always been a deeply personal mission for me because I know what these families are experiencing all too well. My son struggled with school avoidance for many years. He suffered from a severe anxiety disorder, as well as depression. As all parents know, when your child is in pain, you are in pain. Our entire family was challenged and affected. When his school avoidance began around 2009, there was very little information available, and the stigma surrounding mental illness was still strong.

Our school district did not understand school avoidance. The school staff believed my son was purposefully manipulating them and was taking advantage of us, his parents. They delayed providing appropriate support and intervention for several years, wasting valuable time and causing further setbacks.

We consulted multiple mental health professionals until we found an experienced psychiatrist who specialized in helping children with school avoidance and anxiety disorders. That doctor's guidance was a stabilizing support as we continued on a winding road. During those years working toward getting my son back on track, I was fortunate to gain knowledge, guidance, and support from many experts, to whom I am forever grateful. After years of relentless research, advocacy, therapy, and collaboration with dedicated professionals, my son regained his life.

He returned to high school and enjoyed his last two years there. He graduated, went on to university, and started a career he loves. Now he has an active social life and lives with his longtime girlfriend and their three cats. He even has his own health and auto insurance!

You might be thinking, *I'm happy for you, but I can't see that future outcome for my child right now.* I understand. I might have felt the same if I had read this story when my son was in the throes of school avoidance. But I hear from families who are making progress, getting their children back to school, graduating, and continuing a path to independent and fulfilling lives every day.

And real stories of success provide hope. When it comes to school avoidance, hope and belief are not just feelings—they are powerful tools that will propel you forward to get your child where they need to be. Equally important is knowledge. Knowledge is power, and knowledge is necessary!

I wanted to share that hope and hard-won knowledge with other families struggling with school avoidance—because no family or child deserves to go through a journey like ours alone. In 2014, I launched my first website, schoolrefusalhope.org, to help families navigate school avoidance by providing facts, addressing misconceptions, explaining special education rights, and sharing vetted treatment programs.

Today, the School Avoidance Alliance is the premier resource for professional development on the topic of school avoidance across the United States. Our contributions have garnered national attention, with features in prominent publications and media outlets such as *USA Today*, *Education Week*, *The Washington Post*, EdSurge, Fox News, ABC News, and CBS News.

Our flagship courses—"Everything You Need to Know to Get Your Students Back to School" for educators and the "School Avoidance Master Class for Parents"—empower families and have transformed the approach of countless school districts, enhancing their capacity to collaborate using appropriate and effective interventions.

Overcoming school avoidance is a bit more complex than other problems we may face because there isn't just one solution. It's not like an illness or a learning disability, where you get a diagnosis, you get clear next steps and some advice, and then you know what needs to be done. There is almost no definitive advice when it comes to school avoidance, which can make knowing where to start and what to do feel overwhelming and confusing.

The good news is that this book contains all the knowledge you need to help your child. The information presented is derived from evidence-based research, interviews, and conversations with leading clinicians, researchers, educators, advocates, school avoidance families, and a special education attorney representing school districts. I also speak to families and schools daily, so I have a unique vantage point from which I see the common roadblocks, challenges, misconceptions, frustrations, and what does and what does not work.

After you read this book, you will understand:

- **What school avoidance looks like,** including the causes and what first steps you can take toward helping your child.
- **The Four Functions of School Refusal and the School Refusal Assessment Scale,** and how this framework can guide your efforts.

- **How to handle mornings when your child refuses to leave for school** or won't get out of the car at drop-off. Leading school avoidance therapists offer strategies to manage these difficult moments (which are harrowing for parents and children alike).
- **Effective first-line therapeutic approaches** to school avoidance, what your child's therapy should include (and what it shouldn't), and how to respond if your child refuses to attend treatment (a common situation for school-avoidant kids).
- **Who to work with at your school** to ensure proper support, including the role of your school's intervention team.
- **Educational and disability laws** with easy-to-understand information about Section 504 and the Individuals with Disabilities Education Act (IDEA), and how they apply to school avoidance. You'll also learn how most children with school avoidance *do* qualify for a 504 plan, and how many also will be eligible for an Individualized Education Plan (IEP) along with key accommodations, modifications, and services your school can provide to help your child return to school.
- **Insights from a special education attorney** who represents school districts and answers your most pressing questions about proper Section 504 and IDEA compliance. The attorney shares candid insights anonymously, addressing common frustrations that parents share, such as feeling that the school isn't following these laws correctly—an experience some parents describe as feeling like gaslighting.
- **What parental accommodation is,** how it can affect your child's school avoidance, and how to address it. You'll also learn about Supportive Parenting for Anxious Childhood Emotions (SPACE),

a therapy program designed just for parents, from a psychologist who trains clinicians worldwide in this approach.

- **How to support neurodiverse children experiencing school avoidance.** You'll hear from two leading psychologists who help children with autism and school avoidance, as well as get personal insights from a student diagnosed with autism and anxiety, and her experience overcoming school avoidance. Additionally, her mother, now a leading parent coach, provides guidance for families with neurodiverse children.
- **Alternative schooling options,** including online schools and programs. You'll discover insights from dozens of families with school-avoidant children about the different educational paths they explored and what worked best for them.
- **When to consider medication for mental health disorders contributing to school avoidance.** An experienced child psychiatrist provides a balanced perspective on treating anxiety, obsessive compulsive disorder (OCD), and depression, helping you determine whether it might benefit your child and their school avoidance.
- **In-depth accounts from families of school-avoidant children,** including how they supported their child, what they learned throughout the process, and the advice they have for you.

By the end of this book, you will have all the knowledge and guidance—truly, every essential piece of information you need—to guide your child back to their education and life.

CHAPTER 1

School Avoidance

What It Is and Why It Happens

Your life won't always be this way! When your child starts avoiding or refusing school, it can spark a whirlwind of worry, fear, and frustration. These emotions are common among parents navigating this challenging terrain and make sense given the limited information and understanding about the topic. But there's good news: Children with school avoidance are returning to school, and we hear success stories regularly! Yes, even those children who have been out of school for months or even years. Parents who have faced this issue and walked in your shoes always say, "Don't give up, have hope that your child, too, can return to school."

As the founder of the School Avoidance Alliance, I hear these success stories regularly. And before the School Avoidance Alliance, I was like you, a parent trying to figure out the best ways to help my child. My son struggled with school avoidance off and on for about four years. It was a meandering maze to find our way through due to the lack of understanding among professionals and the general public. Once we got my son back to high school and doing well, I built a website and started sharing information. I actually did a lot right to help my child, but there were speed bumps that set us back. This book is about exposing and explaining these obstacles and how you can get through them to get your child back to learning. Today, the School Avoidance Alliance is the premier resource for school avoidance professional development across the United States. Their flagship courses—"Everything You Need to Know to Get Your Students Back to School" for educators and the "School Avoidance Master Class for Parents"—have changed the approach of countless school districts, enhancing their capacity to improve student engagement and success.

Due to the lack of awareness surrounding school avoidance, you might have had no idea what was happening when your child started refusing to attend school. Many families initially feel isolated, thinking they are alone in this struggle. A common frustration is that it can take months or even years to hear the term *school refusal* or *school avoidance*.

Upon learning that there is, in fact, a name for this—"school refusal" or "school avoidance"—parents often experience a profound sense of relief and gratitude. Knowing that this is a recognized issue and that their child isn't alone brings hope and reassurance. School avoidance has been documented since 1932. Dr. David Heyne compiled an extensive list of the different terminology that has been used to describe school avoidance over the years (you can find it at the back of the book in the resources section).

As this research highlights, the issue has been around in one form or another, under the radar for nearly a century. However, as schools reopened after the COVID-19 pandemic, educators saw significant declines in student attendance. For students who already had anxiety disorders, depression, academic frustrations, and limited peer relationships, the COVID school lockdowns reinforced avoidance behaviors, making returning to school more difficult.

This new nationwide crisis of chronic absenteeism has gained a lot of media coverage; however, school avoidance is still largely unknown by the general public. Schools have slowly been introduced to the challenges of school avoidance, but a lot of work remains to be done to make sure every school has been properly educated on school avoidance best practices, evidence-based strategies, and effective interventions.

This book is a resource to help you get your child back to learning and, more importantly, back to their life before their school avoidance. Here, you can find guidance, support, and information to help you and your child navigate this issue.

Dealing with school avoidance can feel isolating, so it may comfort you a little to know that you are not alone in the struggle. Anywhere from hundreds of thousands to several million families are facing the issue of school avoidance.

This is an excellent time to note that school avoidance and school refusal *are the same*. Some researchers and therapists will use the terms *emotionally based school avoidance* or *anxiety-based school avoidance*. (The term *school phobia* is entirely antiquated, so if a therapist is using that term, it may be a sign that they are not up to date with best practices in treating school avoidance.)

What Does School Avoidance Look Like in Children?

When a child refuses to attend school or has difficulty remaining in school all day, we call it school avoidance. Children may show severe emotional discomfort or fear when tasked with going to school. Your child might not display all of these characteristics, but these are signs to look for.

School-avoidant children may:

- Have unusual distress about going to school.
- Cry, scream, or throw tantrums when being awakened for school.
- Pull their blanket over themselves like a cocoon of safety.
- Try to hide from you when it's time to leave.
- Refuse to leave the house to get on the bus or in your car.
- Refuse to get out of your car at school drop-off.
- Go to school but beg you to pick them up during the day.
- Reluctantly go to school only after crying, hiding in their bedroom, having outbursts, or refusing to move.
- Refuse to go in the morning, but will go late every day, usually missing several periods.
- Go to school, but may hide in the bathroom or escape to the nurse or counselor's office.
- Beg you not to make them go back.

School avoidance can start by sporadically refusing to attend school a day or two here and there, over either many years or a shorter time frame. From there, it can slowly increase to where you see a problem and patterns forming. Alternatively, it can start suddenly as refusal with no signs of previous school-avoidant behavior. It isn't uncommon for school avoidance to begin not with absences but with academic changes instead. Early signs may include a pattern of being unable or "forgetting" to do homework, or forgetting or refusing to go for after-school help. Another common sign is a child starting to avoid a specific class. Every child has their own pattern and trajectory of school-avoidant behavior.

Challenges to School Avoidance Awareness

Why aren't more people familiar with such a common issue, and why aren't we doing a better job helping these students? Numerous factors have hindered school avoidance awareness and thwarted improved outcomes, and the factors often feed upon each other:

- **Educators are unaware:** In the past, educators weren't aware of school avoidance and would mislabel struggling students as truant or drop-outs. Educating school professionals about school avoidance is only a recent occurrence prompted by growing chronic absenteeism after the COVID-19 pandemic.
- **Lack of professional development:** Professional development means continued learning. Teachers and school administrators must keep growing their educational knowledge, stay up to date on challenges and improvements, and best address their students' needs. There has been minimal education on school avoidance (other than the School Avoidance Alliance's professional development for schools).
- **It has seemed like a smaller issue than it actually is:** Because there has been little awareness about it, cases have primarily gone undocumented. Schools had no idea about school avoidance and chalked up absenteeism to other causes.
- **Lack of data:** No school data specifically documented a student's absence as school avoidance, so it would be difficult to know how many kids were affected.
- **The stigma of school avoidance:** Because school avoidance is a primarily unknown problem to most of our population, families experiencing it are often blamed and misunderstood.

Understandably, families aren't keen to share that they can't get their kids to go to school. If no one openly talks about school avoidance, how can we learn about its existence?

- **The prevalence of school avoidance:** School avoidance has been challenging to quantify because there isn't a universal way for school districts to report and label absences due to mental health issues and school avoidance. Some school districts in the United States have begun coding absences due to behavioral health issues, and that's a good start. However, it would take a dedicated effort from individual states, our federal government, and other countries to institute such mandates. School refusal occurs among 1 to 7 percent of youth in the general population and 5 to 16 percent of youth seen in clinical settings.

The data we do have for school avoidance comes from global research studies. Researchers share that the number of children dealing with school avoidance is probably much bigger than the research indicates. Dr. Chris Kearney, a leading researcher on school avoidance, author, and professor at the University of Nevada, Las Vegas, points out, "We know that the rates of mental health problems among kids have skyrocketed in recent years, which aligns with the increase in absenteeism. Both trajectories are high, especially post-pandemic, and I feel they are highly correlated."

How We Respond to Children with School Avoidance Is Important

A child with school avoidance may appear so palpably distressed and fearful that it may scare you. Seeing your child this way is difficult and troubling. How you react as a parent may differ and change throughout the school year as well—though your first reaction may be fear and concern, you may find it evolves into anger and frustration over time. Unfortunately, many parents lose control and yell, threaten, and/or break down. No parent is perfect, and getting angry is a natural response. But how we react and respond to our school-avoidant children is important. You will find appropriate responses in Chapter 6 to guide you through morning wake-up and other scenarios that might pop up during the day. Having the tools and words to help your child is vital to their healing.

> "We know that the rates of mental health problems among kids have skyrocketed in recent years, which aligns with the increase in absenteeism. Both trajectories are high, especially post-pandemic, and I feel they are highly correlated."
>
> —DR. CHRIS KEARNEY

Understanding How a School-Avoidant Child Feels

"Paralyzing" and "uncontrollable" are precise and impactful words to accurately describe some of the feelings associated with school avoidance. Families and school staff sometimes interpret the avoidance as defiance, opposition, or manipulation because the child's emotional and fear responses are so powerful that they will do whatever they need to miss school. It's important to understand that children with school avoidance don't want to feel this way. They aren't avoiding school on purpose. They know they are disappointing their parents with their inability to go to school.

Daniel P. Villiers, PhD, co-founder of Mountain Valley Treatment Center and the Anxiety Institute, explains, "School avoidance is a neuro-behavioral condition, neurologically based, behaviorally conditioned, and reinforced. And because in these cases, where a child is controlled by their symptoms right out of the gate, you are working with their shame and guilt, hopelessness, and helplessness."

Dr. Villiers also emphasizes the importance of families responding to school avoidance like a medical condition. "It's crucial to join with the child against the disorder, separating the disorder from the child. Whether it is depression or an anxiety disorder, the school refusal is a symptom that they are victim to—they are not choosing to feel and act this way. They want help, hope, and support, and shouldn't be treated punitively."

Anxiety-Based School Avoidance

Anxiety-based school avoidance is a classic fight-or-flight response. While anxiety is a normal reaction, it becomes problematic when our amygdala (the part of the brain responsible for processing emotions) misinterprets or exaggerates the level of threat, reinforcing fear as a learned and valid response. Avoidance is generally considered a maladaptive behavioral response to excessive fear and anxiety, which in turn sustains anxiety disorder.

Dr. Villiers explains, "Fear is at the heart of all anxiety. If there isn't a fear, it's not anxiety. For it to be anxiety-based school avoidance, it must be dominated by fear, which drives increasing dependence on avoidance and escape, physical symptoms, physiological symptoms, or psychosomatic cognitive symptoms—these are often visible, but don't have to be. It's got to have this AFA cycle as we call it—anxiety, fear, avoidance cycle—that dominates the child's life, and you can clearly link it to why they are avoiding school specifically."

> "It's crucial to join with the child against the disorder, separating the disorder from the child. Whether it is depression or an anxiety disorder, the school refusal is a symptom that they are victim to—they are not choosing to feel and act this way. They want help, hope, and support, and shouldn't be treated punitively."
>
> —DR. DANIEL VILLIERS

The anxiety-avoidance cycle refers to the thoughts, feelings, and behaviors triggered by a perceived threat. When our brain perceives danger, the body prepares to flee to keep us safe. Avoidance involves anything we do to escape from the perceived threats, providing short-term relief but increasing anxiety over time. The more anxious we get, the more we avoid, and the more we avoid, the more anxious we get. By avoiding the anxiety triggers, we teach the brain that avoidance is the only path to relief.

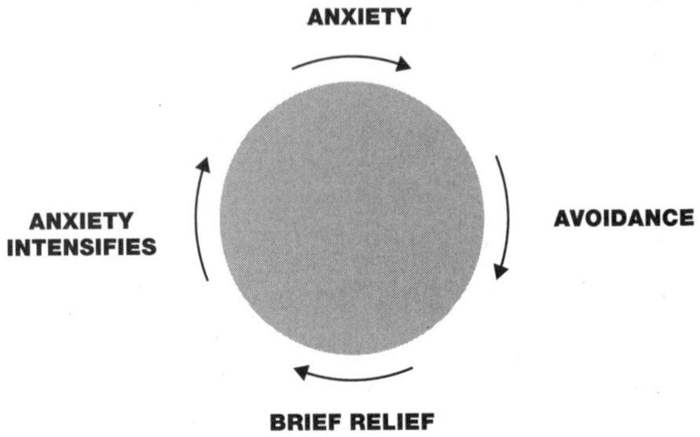

In Chapter 2, you will learn from psychologists how to break this cycle of avoidance.

The Definition of School Avoidance

The operational definition of school refusal, established by Dr. Ian Berg of the University of Leeds in 1997, offers a precise set of criteria to identify school avoidance in children. This definition remains widely utilized today. To be classified as school avoidance, the following criteria must be met:

- Less than 80 percent attendance recorded over two consecutive weeks (excluding legitimate absences).
- The presence of an anxiety disorder as identified in *Diagnostic and Statistical Manual of Mental Disorders*, 5th Edition (DSM-5), excluding obsessive-compulsive disorder (OCD) and post-traumatic stress disorder (PTSD).
- Parents can account for the child's whereabouts on the days marked by school absence.
- No concurrent DSM-5 conduct disorder (although mild forms of oppositional defiance are permitted).

- Parents must be committed to helping the child achieve total school attendance except for legitimate reasons.

Spotting the Signs

When it comes to your children, your instincts and gut feelings are usually right—so trust yourself. Try not to talk yourself out of these observations. It's not uncommon to avoid or deny the issue of school avoidance because it can feel overwhelming, and you may not know where to find help. Picking up this book is a great step forward. You are proactively seeking guidance for the well-being of your child and your family. Be proud of yourself. It may not seem like a big deal, but it is! Not all parents take this step forward, investing their time to become the best advocate possible for their child.

Your observations are as important as the clinical definition when determining if your child is experiencing school avoidance. Here are some signs that may point to school avoidance:

- Your child is not missing a lot of school days yet, but they are starting to have trouble getting up and out to school.
- Your child is going to school, but only after crying or breaking down as they get ready for school.
- Your child is chronically tardy.
- From one day to the next, you don't know if your child will go to school, get to school on time, or remain in school the whole day.
- Your child's reluctance to attend school is causing stress within your family or daily life.
- Your child's normal daily activities (and possibly yours as well) are negatively affected.
- Your child is falling behind in schoolwork.

Your child's challenges are negatively affecting their ability to participate in, engage with, or do schoolwork to gain an education. In special education and disability law, this is referred to as "ability to access their education." Despite all this, your school may report that your child appears fine and that they don't see any signs of trouble. This can lead you to question yourself and what you observe at home. It's important to understand that children in distress often hide their genuine emotions or fears from peers and teachers at school. Your child feels safe at home, which is where they can show their real distress. If you feel there is a problem, there probably is. Again, trust your gut.

What Causes School Avoidance?

School avoidance or refusal is not a clinical diagnosis; it is a symptom of an emotional disorder or other underlying issue that drives avoidance. Therefore, there is no diagnostic code for school avoidance in the *Diagnostic and Statistical Manual of Mental Disorders*, 5th Edition (DSM-5), which is the authoritative source for defining and classifying mental health disorders. The absence of school avoidance in the DSM presents an additional challenge, as it allows room for some to dismiss the issue.

One of the most challenging aspects for parents is determining the cause of the avoidance. It's common for children experiencing school avoidance to be unable to explain why it is happening.

Along with gathering information by talking with your school and your child (if they are willing to communicate), making your own observations is crucial. A key first step is to use the School Refusal Assessment Scale—Revised (SRAS-R), discussed later in this chapter, to help identify the root cause of the school avoidance.

The Four Functions of School Refusal

Given the many factors contributing to school avoidance, it can feel overwhelming to decipher what is happening to your child. The Four Functions of School Refusal, originally developed by Dr. Chris Kearney and his colleague Dr. Wendy Silverman, provide a foundational framework for understanding the underlying cause (or function) of a child's school refusal. This model aids mental health professionals and schools in determining the best course of action.

School Refusal Assessment: Focus on Function

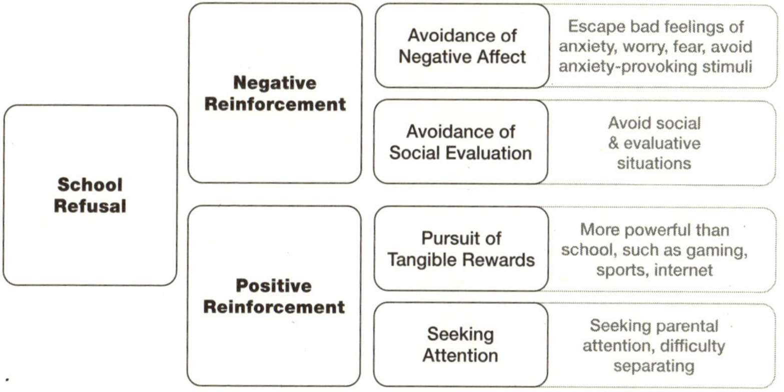

The Four Functions of School Refusal

Is your child avoiding school due to negative reinforcement (functions one and two) or seeking positive reinforcement (functions three and four)?

The four functions of school refusal are as follows:

FUNCTION 1

To avoid objects or situations at school that cause the child unpleasant physical symptoms or general distress; for example:

- Being on the school bus
- Walking in the hallways
- Being on the playground
- Being in the lunchroom
- Sitting in the classroom
- Fear of not keeping up in class
- Distress from difficulty doing schoolwork because of a learning difference
- Interactions with school staff (teachers, principals, etc.)

FUNCTION 2

To avoid social or evaluative situations that are uncomfortable for the child (school-related performance tasks); for example:

- Tests
- Reading aloud to the class
- Speaking or presenting in front of others
- Athletic performance in gym class
- The playground
- Recreational school sports

FUNCTION 3

To receive attention from a parent or significant other; for example:

- Difficulty separating from a parent, sibling, or caregiver
- Feeling like they are needed by a parent

FUNCTION 4

To gain tangible rewards that make staying home more enjoyable than going to school. In some cases, children may initially avoid school to escape negative feelings (functions one and two) and later discover the positive rewards of staying home, such as the comfort of being in a safe space with all their favorite things; for example:

- Staying home to play online games
- Spending time online or watching movies
- Spending time with a friend who is also not in school

The School Refusal Assessment Scale (SRAS-R)

To better assess which of these functions might apply to a particular child, Dr. Kearney and Dr. Silverman developed the School Refusal Assessment Scale (SRAS). A revised version (SRAS-R) was later created in collaboration with Dr. Anne Marie Albano. This questionnaire uses a Likert scale to help establish the underlying function of the child's school refusal, allowing mental health professionals, schools, and families to determine the appropriate course of action. Once the SRAS-R is scored, the function with the highest mean score is considered the primary cause of the child's school avoidance.

You can find both versions (for the parent and the child), on page 249 of the resources section, along with an explanation and example of how to score them.

Dr. Kearney explains, "One mistake people make regarding the functional model is applying it to all cases. But it was originally designed for more acute cases, primarily for cases that have been ongoing for less than a calendar year. Once the situation becomes more chronic, other contextual factors come into play and the scope must be broadened. While the functional approach is still valid, it's best applied to cases of less than one calendar year. Once you get past one calendar year, which is really two academic years, the problem gets a lot more complex."

Common Causes Associated with School Avoidance

According to the research and real-life accounts, school avoidance is often linked to mental health challenges, such as anxiety disorders, depression, obsessive-compulsive disorder (OCD), or post-traumatic stress disorder (PTSD). Learning differences, such as dyslexia, attention deficit hyperactivity disorder (ADHD), slow processing, and developmental differences (e.g., autism spectrum disorder), are also common contributors.

School avoidance behaviors often occur alongside mental health challenges or undiagnosed learning differences. In addition to cases where learning differences are diagnosed but not adequately addressed with appropriate interventions or accommodations, school avoidance may occur.

ADHD and School Avoidance

Studies have found that adolescents with ADHD have higher rates of absenteeism compared to neurotypical peers. Among those with ADHD, "school aversion" is a common reason for absence, suggesting that difficulty concentrating and lack of adequate support in school contribute to avoidance.

Imagine how difficult it must feel for a child who has ADHD, dyslexia, or slow processing in the classroom. They may struggle to keep up, grasp concepts, or complete assignments, leading to feelings of inadequacy and anxiety. What if the teacher calls on them, and they have no idea what's going on? What if they must work with classmates but cannot contribute? It's easy to see how these experiences could feel overwhelming and awful.

Co-Occurring Conditions

Anxiety Disorders	Learning Differences	Anxiety Disorders
Panic disorder	Processing speed disorders	Depression
Social anxiety	Dyslexia	Trauma-related disorder
Separation anxiety	Dyscalculia (math dyslexia, distinct from math anxiety)	Perfectionism
OCD	Disorder of written expression	ADD/ADHD
Specific phobia	Executive functioning deficits	Bullying
Generalized anxiety disorder	ADD/ADHD	Prolonged absence due to injury or illness
Selective mutism (difficulty speaking in certain social situations)		Death or illness of parent or pet
Emetophobia (fear of vomiting)		Changes in class or school
		A new teacher
		An intimidating or toxic teacher
		Perceptions of inclusion toward anyone and marginalized communities (LGBTQ+, English language learners, people of color, unhoused families)
		Neurodivergence (e.g., autism spectrum disorder)
		Feeling unsafe at school
		A new school

School Avoidance and Oppositional Defiant Disorder (ODD)

It is important to note that school avoidance is sometimes misinterpreted as oppositional defiant disorder (ODD). Your child's avoidance may seem oppositional or defiant. However, ODD has more severe behaviors characterized by violent outbursts, resistance to rules, and a preference for spiteful behavior that would be apparent before any signs of school avoidance. Children with ODD may have school refusal behaviors, but only a small percentage of kids with school avoidance also have ODD.

Bullying and School Avoidance

If bullying isn't properly addressed by the school or resolved to your child's satisfaction, school can understandably become an uncomfortable place for them. It's crucial for parents to act swiftly and decisively to ensure the school responds appropriately.

Dr. Karen Cassiday, PhD, ACT, owner and managing director of the Anxiety Treatment Center of Greater Chicago, recommends teaching students, parents, and educators how to diffuse bullying while building resilience in students. She endorses the Bullies to Buddies methods developed by psychologist Izzy Kalman, which teach ways to respond to a bully that immediately decrease the incidence of bullying and strengthen the victim's resilience by empowering them to solve the problem. Information about Dr. Kalman's approach can be found online and is incorporated into the videos and presentations of Brooks Gibbs, a resilience educator with a PhD in social psychology.

Your child's sense of safety is the top priority. Feeling safe at school through a positive school climate and culture and being empowered with problem-solving skills are essential for their well-being.

Your child may experience one or more of the circumstances listed in the "Co-Occurring Conditions" chart earlier in this chapter. But as you will see in the next section, school-related factors can also play a part.

Characteristics of School Settings Associated with School Avoidance

Until recently, the causes of school avoidance focused on aspects relating to the child's challenges or deficits (individual factors) and parental factors. However, current research has identified school-related factors as significant contributing factors to school avoidance.

Several triggers, not related to disorders or learning differences, can also exist. These triggers are often brought on or exacerbated by school-related factors, such as:

- Limited friendships at school
- Changes in the friend group
- Outgrowing a friend group or no longer relating to them
- Pressure to perform and excel
- High-demand courses like honors and IB (International Baccalaureate) programs
- Increased workload (e.g., transitioning from elementary to middle school)
- Experiencing trauma in school
- Absences due to physical illness
- Lack of meaningful relationships with school staff
- Fear of unstructured time, concerns about school safety, or lingering fears from the COVID-19 pandemic
- Social challenges (e.g., victimization, bullying, difficulty making friends, isolation)

- Perceptions of inclusion toward anyone and marginalized communities (LGBTQ+), English language learners (ELL), people of color, unhoused families
- School culture and climate
- Lack of mental health awareness and support

A child's emotional experience in the classroom and school environment can significantly impact their ability to function at school. Relationships with teachers, teacher support, fear of the teacher, and a noisy or unpredictable classroom all play a role in school refusal. A qualitative interview study among parents of children who refused school highlighted the importance of classroom predictability for attendance. Additionally, a lack of classroom structure and organization has been linked to nonattendance and even dropping out.

The Most Influential School-Related Factors Predicting High School Graduation

On the flip side, certain factors help children stay connected and remain in school. Positive student-teacher relationships, characterized by respectful interactions, teacher interest in students, and student confidence in teacher competence, contribute significantly to continued enrollment. Smaller schools, where teachers and students can form closer relationships, also play a positive role.

Out-of-school programs, such as community service, social-emotional learning, and academic enrichment, have long-lasting benefits for children struggling with school avoidance. Extracurricular activities, community service, and career or technical education opportunities help keep children engaged and enrolled.

New and Welcome Perspectives

Research on school avoidance is shifting away from blaming children or parents. Experts now acknowledge that absenteeism has broader influencing factors; so resolving and improving attendance issues are more evenly distributed among all participants and collaborators.

Stakeholders now understand that interconnected risk/protective factors contribute to school avoidance. Examples include disability/academic achievement (student level), psychopathology/academic involvement (caregiver level), residential movement/cohesion (family level), victimization/positive norms (peer level), negative/positive climate quality (school level), neighborhood violence/safe avenues to school (community level), and structural economic inequalities/well-financed educational agencies.

The research and real-life data show that negative interventions (punitive measures), paradoxically, exacerbate school absenteeism and are disproportionately and perniciously applied to vulnerable student groups. Examples include exclusionary discipline (e.g., arrests, expulsion, and suspension) and zero tolerance laws that often focus on deprivation of resources (e.g., via fines or court involvement).

While this guidance away from punishment is promising, it's slow to reach stakeholders such as schools and truancy courts. Parents may feel judged, misunderstood, or blamed, which can make the experience isolating and frightening. People unfamiliar with school avoidance often underestimate the distress and disruption it can cause.

Getting support from others who understand exactly how you feel is essential in helping you maintain your strength, advocacy, and sanity. You didn't cause your child's school avoidance, and it's important to remember that. The School Avoidance Alliance's website (schoolavoidance.org) offers a supportive community for families experiencing similar issues.

Parental Disagreement and School Avoidance

Another unfortunate reality is that parents often disagree on how to handle their child's school avoidance. One parent may feel the child is manipulating the other, labeling them as weak, coddling, or indulgent. Their partner may respond with frustration, anger, or even punishment. It's important to avoid letting your child overhear these conflicting views, as it can exacerbate their anxiety.

Additionally, if you have other children in your home, they may feel neglected or overwhelmed by their sibling's challenges. Don't be too hard on yourself. Balancing family life while supporting a school-avoidant child is no easy task.

Early Interventions Lead to the Best Outcomes

All the research and real-life experience on school avoidance emphasize the importance of early intervention. Prolonged absence reinforces avoidant behavior: The longer a child is out of school, the harder it becomes for them to return.

It may sound simple enough: See a problem, get help. However, due to the lack of awareness surrounding school avoidance, signs are often missed, and appropriate responses are often delayed.

Trust Your Instincts

School avoidance can feel overwhelming, and it's normal to question your instincts or delay action. But when it comes to your kids, your instincts are usually right.

So, listen to them—you are your child's greatest advocate.

CHAPTER 2

Effective Therapies

Exploring Treatment Options

When a child begins avoiding school, it can leave parents feeling bewildered and uncertain. Since the issue isn't commonly discussed in the media, in our schools, and among friends and family, it can be hard to know what steps to take. After informing the school, a sensible next step is to rule out any medical problems and consult a mental health professional.

For children who report physical symptoms—like headaches, stomach pain, nausea, or vomiting—it's crucial to consult your pediatrician to address any potential health concerns.

According to Harvard Medical School, "The gut-brain connection is no joke; it can link anxiety to stomach problems and vice versa. The brain has a direct effect on the stomach and intestines. This connection goes both ways. A troubled intestine can send signals to the brain, just as a troubled brain can send signals to the gut. Therefore, a person's stomach or intestinal distress can be the cause *or* the product of anxiety, stress, or depression. That's because the brain and the gastrointestinal (GI) system are intimately connected."

Mental health issues are often at the root of school avoidance, so consulting a mental health provider is always a good idea. There are many different kinds of mental health professionals who can help, such as psychologists, social workers, counselors, and psychiatrists. If you're unsure which type of professional to consult, the National Alliance on Mental Health provides detailed descriptions to help you make an informed choice.

A mental health provider can determine whether your child has a diagnosable disorder contributing to or causing their school avoidance. They should be able to help you and your child understand the issue and provide a treatment plan. A good therapist should be accessible, act as a partner in your child's care, and agree to communicate regularly with your school as you work with them to help your child. You can consider them a part of your School Avoidance Team.

Modes of Therapy

When addressing school avoidance, selecting the right therapeutic approach is crucial. Not all therapies are equally effective, and understanding the different modes of therapy can empower families to make informed decisions.

Cognitive Behavioral Therapy (CBT)

Cognitive behavioral therapy (CBT) has the most scientific support in the treatment of school refusal. Over two thousand studies demonstrate that CBT can help people with a wide range of health and mental health conditions, as well as quality of life concerns. CBT is a practical, structured approach that teaches clients to recognize their thoughts, understand how they affect their feelings, and examine their behaviors, making it highly applicable in real life. Typically, CBT is a short-term treatment lasting around three to six months, but children with school avoidance may require longer treatment timelines.

Unlike traditional talk therapy, CBT is more goal-oriented and involves actively working on thoughts and behaviors. Research shows that CBT can be effective for children starting around age seven and can be adapted for children as young as three using age-appropriate techniques, ensuring its suitability for children of various ages.

The guiding principle of CBT is that our thoughts influence our feelings, which in turn influence our behavior. CBT focuses on identifying unhelpful and inaccurate thoughts that lead to negative emotions and maladaptive behaviors. This is often referred to as the CBT triangle: thoughts, feelings, and behaviors.

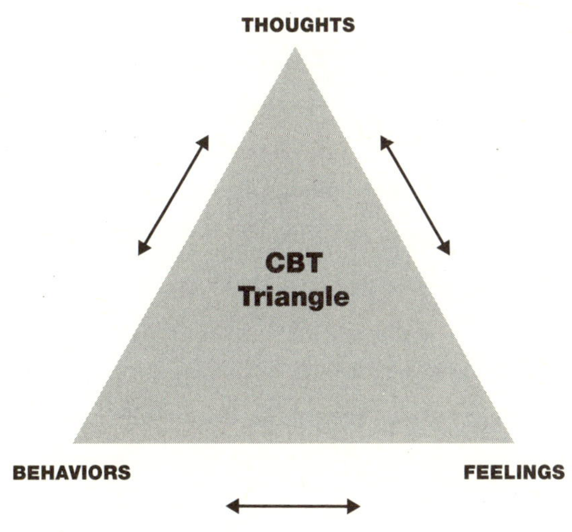

UNDERSTANDING CBT

- **Cognitive:** Refers to the process of acquiring knowledge and understanding through thought, experience, and senses.
- **Behavioral:** Refers to a person's actions and responses. In CBT, this includes a wide range of behaviors—positive, negative, and neutral. School avoidance is both cognitive and behavioral because you can't have one without the other.
- **Therapy:** The treatment and intervention provided by a mental health professional to address a problem or disorder.

KEY COMPONENTS OF CBT

- **Psychoeducation:** This is essential to any therapy. Psychoeducation involves educating the patient about their mental health condition to help them understand what they are experiencing and how to seek proper support. Psychoeducation for CBT should include an explanation of how treatment works, what to expect, and the roles of both you and the therapist. Therapists may use visual aids or graphics to promote understanding of therapeutic concepts.
- **Automatic thoughts:** These pop into your head all day, coming up suddenly without effort. The National Science Foundation estimates that a person has twelve thousand to sixty thousand thoughts daily. Automatic negative thoughts (ANTs) are automatic thoughts that trigger negative, distorted thinking. For children with school avoidance, ANTs can include thoughts like "I am stupid," "No one likes me at school," "I'm going to fail my test," or "I'll get bullied if I go to school." These thoughts are often irrational and exaggerated, but they can significantly impact a child's behavior and emotions.
- **Unhelpful thinking styles (cognitive distortions):** These are biased ways of thinking that can distort perception. Therapists often refer

to these as "thinking traps" because the mind may present distorted thoughts as true.

Common thinking traps include overgeneralization, personalization, filtering, all-or-nothing thinking, catastrophizing, jumping to conclusions, emotional reasoning, discounting the positive, and "should" statements.

A study on students with generalized anxiety disorder revealed that 91.4 percent of worrisome thoughts did not come true and 30.1 percent turned out better than expected.

CBT TECHNIQUES

- **Homework:** A core component of CBT is homework. Therapists understand that the thought of homework might deter a school-avoidant child, so many use terms like "skills practice" or "action plans." This work helps clients recognize and examine their thoughts, feelings, and behaviors. Common homework includes thought records to notice automatic thoughts, identify thinking traps, fact-check thoughts, and cognitive restructuring to challenge and reframe negative thoughts.
- **Problem-solving approach:** CBT uses a problem-solving approach in which the therapist and client work together to address the child's school avoidance within the CBT framework. This collaborative approach underscores the therapist's important role in providing support and guidance.

CBT IN PRACTICE

CBT isn't just a theoretical approach; it's highly practical and focuses on real-life applications. Therapists work closely with children to practice new skills and strategies in a supportive environment. These applications are vital in helping children translate what they learn in therapy into their everyday lives.

› **Coping skills:** CBT also teaches children coping skills to manage anxiety and stress. These can include deep breathing exercises, mindfulness practices, and relaxation techniques. These skills are essential for helping children manage their anxiety at the moment they experience it and can be useful throughout their lives.

Exposure Therapy for School Avoidance

Although we often discuss exposure therapy as a separate treatment, it is technically considered part of CBT. However, not all CBT therapists practice or are experienced in using exposure therapy. Most experts dedicated to school avoidance agree that exposure is a critical component of treatment, helping children return to school and achieve sustainable, long-term results.

"In exposure therapy, clients are asked to confront the situations they fear, starting with the least frightening situations, mastering them, then moving to more difficult situations, mastering those, and so on until the most difficult situations no longer interfere with the client's life," explains Dr. Anne Marie Albano, founder of the Columbia University Clinic for Anxiety and Related Disorders in New York City. "The child remains in each level of anxiety long enough for the anxiety to decrease. They learn that they can manage the anxiety caused by exposure. Gradual exposure continues until they are comfortable being in school again."

Dr. Albano considers the goals of exposure therapy are to:

- Provide experience performing in and managing difficult situations.
- Practice and refine skills.
- Gather evidence to refute anxious thoughts.
- Habituate and tolerate anxiety.

Unfortunately, many parents dealing with school avoidance are unaware of exposure therapy. This could be due to its limited coverage in mainstream media and the fact that many mental health professionals do not utilize it in their practice. Ideally, an experienced exposure therapist would collaborate with you and your school, but access to these therapists can be limited due to a shortage of mental health professionals specializing in exposure therapy.

Don't worry—even if you don't have a therapist, your school does have professionals such as school psychologists, social workers, counselors, and sometimes outside mental health providers they can bring in to help you work on a reintegration plan based on exposure therapy.

The exposures will eventually progress to entering the school building. You and your school will need to strategize when and where your child's first exposures will take place and which room they will go to, with whom, and for how long. Additionally, you and your school will develop a plan for when and how to reintroduce academic work.

In the next section, we explore exposure therapy in greater depth and learn more from Dr. Dina Nunziato, the chief clinical officer of the Anxiety Institute in Greenwich, Connecticut. The Anxiety Institute offers intensive outpatient treatment programs and customized services for children, adolescents, and young adults dealing with anxiety disorders, OCD, and school avoidance. Dr. Nunziato has over twenty years of experience helping young adults in clinical and educational settings, specializing in cognitive behavioral treatment for anxiety and related disorders. Her research includes evidence-based mindfulness techniques for anxiety management, academic success, and emotional well-being.

Learning Theories Behind Exposure Therapy with Dr. Dina Nunziato

Exposure therapy gives people the structure to face their fears, but what truly makes it work are the learning processes that help reshape their response to anxiety over time.

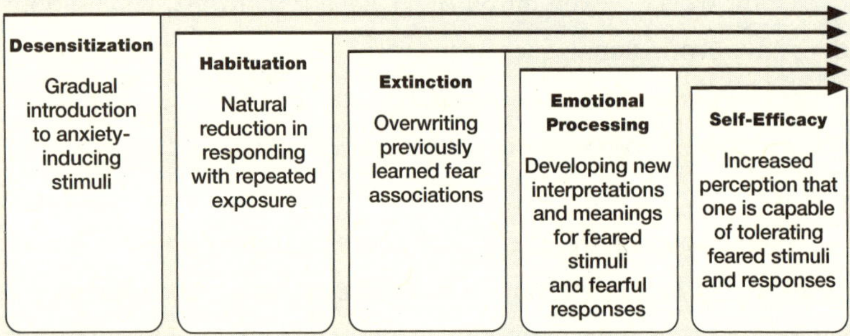

Replicated with permission by the Anxiety Institute

Desensitization is a gradual introduction to the stimuli that create the anxiety. **Habituation** is the natural reduction in response to repeated exposure. So, with repeated exposure, we create desensitization, habituation, and, ultimately, the conditions for new learning to occur. By learning new ways to experience the feared stimuli, our clients can then create new associations between stimulus and response. When clients have enough experiences to establish new neural pathways, these pathways become the new default mode for our previously learned associations.

Ultimately, new **emotional processing** occurs, allowing clients to develop new interpretations and meanings of the stimuli. And then, finally, increased **self-efficacy** is established, with the confidence that one can tolerate the feared stimuli and any resulting responses.

Exposure therapy is a critically important strategy for anxiety-related school refusal. It's about deliberately facing the fear, leaning into the feared situation, desensitizing, and progressing to new learning and emotional reprocessing.

So, in terms of exposure-focused CBT for anxiety-related school refusal, we're going to identify the triggers:

* What triggers the anxiety?
* Are the triggers specific people, places, or situations?

We will go through and look very methodically at identifying the triggers. Then, once we have the triggers in place, we will look at an individualized treatment plan. The treatment plan is between the parent or the caregiver, the provider, the clinicians, and the school. The child or the adolescent is at the center of this.

Once we understand the variables of influence, **we create a fear hierarchy**. We look at the situations that trigger fear, we look at some low-level fears, and that's where we'll start developing the exposure work. We'll gradually work our way up.

Exposure Hierarchy, aka Anxiety Ladder

To gauge the child's distress, the therapist often uses a **Subjective Units of Distress Scale (SUDS)**. Each item in the hierarchy receives a SUDS rating (0–100), ranking items from least distressing (0) to most distressing (100). We start at the bottom and the exposures are customized to the child's triggers and goals, from easiest to hardest.

The goal of exposure is to gradually expose the child to whatever it is that they are avoiding, which helps them reduce their anxiety and make progress toward returning to school.

School Attendance Hierarchy

Fear Thermometer (SUDS*)

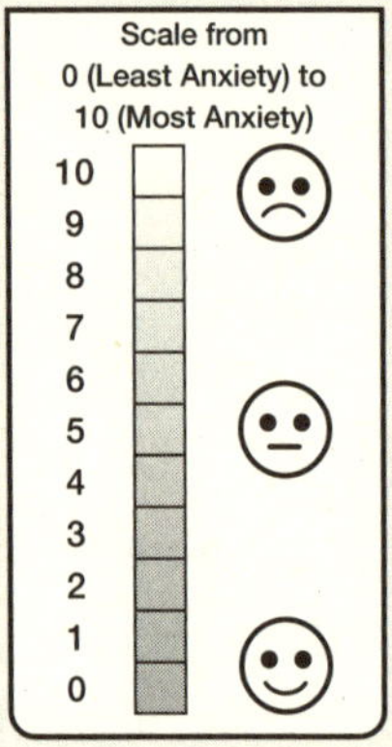

Scale from 0 (Least Anxiety) to 10 (Most Anxiety)

10
9
8
7
6
5
4
3
2
1
0

School Refusal Fear Hierarchy

Situation	SUDS
Spending a whole day in school	10
Spending 2 hours at school	8
Going to select classes, rest of day in library	7
Go to school in a.m.; sit in library	7
Visit a teacher at school	5
Meet with guidance counselor	4
Talk to a teacher on the phone	3
Regulate morning routine	2

* Subjective Units of Distress
Chart replicated courtesy of Dr. Anne Marie Albano

Gradual Exposure

If we rapidly increase anxiety, it motivates the urge to escape and inhibits new learning. We know that, so we avoid doing that. A common misconception is that our anxiety will continue to increase catastrophically the longer we are exposed to it, and the more and more afraid we will get.

But the reality is that over time, as you're exposed to anxiety-inducing stimuli, you can learn to lean into it. The gradual exposure to the feared object or situation can result in habituation and, ultimately, reduced fear. Fear often recedes faster with repeated exposure. We also want to ensure that we're doing this in a gradual way so that we're not exposing the client to their greatest fear immediately. If we move too quickly, the client will shut down, go into complete freeze mode, and we won't be able to do the work.

How Anxiety Peaks, Then Drops: The Power of Repeated Exposure

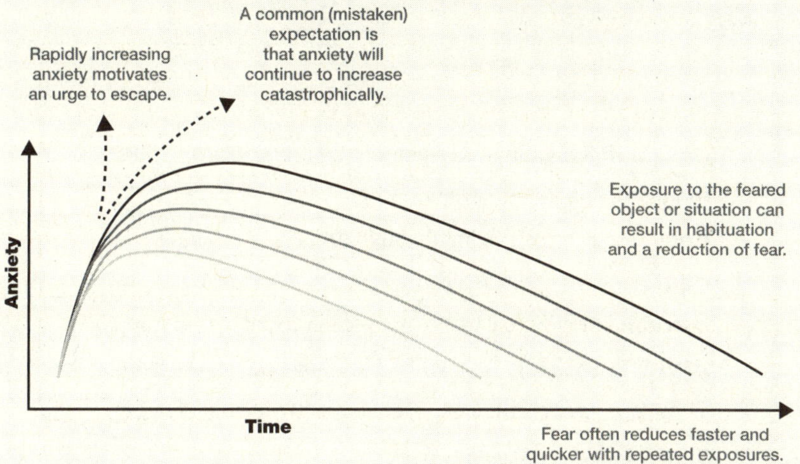

The dotted lines at the top illustrate how we tend to perceive anxiety—rising sharply and spiraling out of control. In contrast, the solid lines demonstrate how anxiety actually decreases over time with gradual exposure. From the darkest top line to the lightest bottom line, the image shows that repeated exposure helps anxiety dissipate more quickly, reinforcing the idea that each experience builds resilience.

A simplified example of some gradual exposures may be:

* Going to the school parking lot.
* Getting out of the car.
* Walking into the building.
* Walking the hallways.

So, the exposures are graduated, moving at the client's own pace.

We're not going to ask the client to do anything that they're not able to do. However, we will ask them to try to stay at their growing edge. We don't want to ask them to do something that's not causing them any anxiety at all, because then we're not doing the work. Instead, we always want to ask them to push themselves and to continue getting a little bit further each time we do this.

Exposures *may* begin as:

* **Imaginal:** Imagining or remembering anxiety-provoking thoughts, images, or situations.
* **Conversational:** Talking through anxiety-provoking experiences in great detail.
* **Virtual:** Using virtual reality with scenarios of feared stimuli.
* **In vivo (real life):** "In vivo" is Latin for "within the living." These are your real-life exposures directly facing a feared object, situation, or activity.

Here are some more examples of possible exposures for school avoidance:

* Talking to school personnel
* Gradually having students work with their guidance counselor or their support team
* Gradually building time in school

Again, these are simplified examples (the time frames listed here are random for example purposes and should not be interpreted as a suggested exposure plan) since each child starts and progresses at their own pace according to their ability to move through habituation to self-efficacy, as explained above.

* Perhaps this week, we're going to attend one class.
* Maybe next week, we're going to attend three.
* Perhaps we do it by the hour, going to school for an hour today.
* Two days from now, you're going to go in for two hours a day.

Each time a new exposure is achieved and repeated, we reinforce new learning and strengthen the new neural pathways between the previously feared stimulus and the new response. The eventual goal is for a child to attend school, even when they're anxious, and be able to tolerate the feelings of anxiety without engaging in compensatory behaviors (avoiding or escaping the situation).

Developmentally, you also need to figure out where your child is; with younger children, you can take a more parent-directed approach, utilizing age-appropriate language and goals. Typically, with younger children, there's greater family involvement and more focus on adult-determined goals and positive reinforcement. For adolescents and young adults, who are in the separation-individuation phase of development, it is best to collaborate with them to think through what exposures make sense. By doing this, you provide the adolescent the ability to co-develop exposures and optimize their buy-in and motivation for change.

—Dr. Dina Nunziato

Identifying a Common Misstep

Sometimes, school professionals are aware of exposure therapy but haven't been trained on how to use it effectively for their school-avoidant students. They may have good intentions, thinking they are helping, but when exposure is used incorrectly, it can cause setbacks.

In these scenarios, the school builds a reintegration plan for your child, but it isn't based on the child's individual needs, isn't fluid, and doesn't follow the core tenets of exposure, as previously mentioned.

An example of an *incorrect* plan to return to school developed by your school may look like this:

- Monday: Go to school, meet with the school counselor, and sit in their office for an hour.
- Tuesday: Attend period 1.
- Wednesday: Attend periods 1 and 2.
- Thursday: Attend half a day.
- Friday: Attend a full day.

Unfortunately, these types of rushed and misused plans are often given to parents.

When doing exposure/reintegration, the exposures must start and progress according to your child's *present level of functioning*. This refers to the level your child is at in daily life functioning. For example, some children cannot leave their rooms, while others cannot leave their houses or do not want to see friends or extended family members. Some children can leave their homes and still see friends. Some are out of school but able to do their schoolwork at home, while others cannot. Some children won't get into the car to go to school, and some will get in the car but won't get out when they arrive. With this in mind, the first exposure for each child has a different starting point. If a child is not leaving their room, their first exposure might be to just come out of their room or perhaps spend time in a room they share with other family members in their home. Not all first exposures will be related to school.

Mental health professionals often call this "meeting the child where they are at." The exposure reintegration plans must be created to meet the child's current level of functioning. The reintegration plan will then be continually evaluated and changed according to the child's ability to reach habituation, extinction, and self-efficacy for that one exposure.

Each child is different, so the time frames and steps will vary. Sometimes, parents or schools are eager to get the student back to class and a full academic load, so it's important to remain mindful of that and ensure that those feelings don't interfere with a realistic plan. Slow and gradual is the way to go.

Finding a Qualified CBT and Exposure Therapist

When seeking a qualified cognitive behavioral and exposure therapist, it is essential to note that therapists and psychologists vary in training, expertise, and experience. Not all therapists who practice CBT are experienced in exposure therapy, so it's crucial to ask.

Here are some questions to consider when choosing a therapist:

- Ask them where they were trained and educated in CBT and exposure therapy.
- Ask them to explain how they utilize CBT and exposure in their practice. They should incorporate key aspects of CBT, such as automatic thought records, thought distortions, and cognitive restructuring. Sometimes, therapists may say they use CBT but only incorporate parts of it, like mindfulness and relaxation skills. Be sure to ask specific questions.

- For exposure therapy, ask how they incorporate exposures with school-avoidant children and make sure they use in-vivo (real-life) exposures. Experienced exposure therapists share that, if all of your child's visits are only in the therapist's office, they are not doing exposure therapy.
- Strongly consider meeting with the therapist alone or with your partner first to ensure that you are confident in their ability to help your child with school avoidance. Getting school-avoidant children to a therapist's office isn't always easy, so you should do whatever is possible to determine the therapist's suitability.
- Ask how often and when the therapist plans to speak with you privately.
- After your child's first or second visit, ask for a treatment plan.
- If you don't feel confident in the therapist, don't hesitate to seek out another professional.

Also, many more therapists (including exposure therapists) now offer online sessions, which may make it easier for your child to see a mental health professional. Telehealth therapy for kids is more available than ever, with many therapists offering virtual sessions that are covered by private insurance and Medicaid.

Why Is My Child Refusing Therapy?

It's common for families experiencing school avoidance to also face the challenge of children refusing therapy. Going to therapy can be challenging for both adults and children due to stigma, fear, and misunderstandings about how counseling works. Here are some common reasons children might resist therapy and how parents can address them:

- **Belief they don't need help:** Kids might not recognize they have a problem or may find comfort in their current state. Parents should ask the child what they want to achieve from therapy and align therapy goals with the child's motivations.
- **Shame:** Children might feel ashamed if therapy is used as a punishment. Parents should explain therapy as a safe space to talk about worries and feelings.
- **Fear of vulnerability:** Children may be uncomfortable with their emotions. Therapy can help them navigate these feelings, and parents should emphasize that seeking help is a sign of strength.
- **Parental engagement:** Therapy is more effective when parents are involved and supportive. Parents should encourage their child to use the skills learned in therapy.
- **Embarrassment:** Teenagers might feel embarrassed about needing help. Parents should frame therapy as a normal and helpful process.
- **Defensiveness:** Teens may feel judged and resist therapy. Parents should reassure them that therapy is a judgment-free space.
- **Confidentiality concerns:** Teens might worry about privacy. Parents should explain that therapy sessions are confidential.
- **Challenges in therapy:** Therapy can be hard work. Parents should support their child through difficult sessions and provide feedback to the therapist.
- **Uncertainty about what to talk about:** Parents should reassure their child that the therapist will guide the conversation. By understanding and addressing these concerns, parents can help their children feel more comfortable and willing to engage in therapy.

What Should You Do if Your Child Refuses Therapy?

Kids may want to avoid talking about their experiences, and for those with social anxiety, interacting with or even being seen by another person can feel overwhelming.

Clinicians treating children with school avoidance often suggest that parents visit the therapist themselves if their child refuses therapy. This is a worthwhile and valuable starting point. The therapist can offer support, understanding, and acknowledgment of your child's school avoidance. They'll also provide psychoeducation to help you better understand what your child is experiencing and to communicate more effectively with your child.

A therapist can give you strategies to use at home, as well as advice on how to elicit the help of your school. Often, after several sessions, your demeanor and responses to your child will improve, which can help them feel more understood and supported. Over time, your child may agree to meet with the therapist themself, especially if they notice positive changes in your responses and understanding.

Another effective therapeutic option is Supportive Parenting for Anxious Childhood Emotions (SPACE), a parent-only therapy covered in Chapter 9.

How Do You Know if Your Child Is Engaging in Therapy?

It's sometimes hard for parents to tell if their child is engaged or is making progress in therapy. You want your child to improve, and you are investing time and money in their treatment, so it's crucial to ensure that they're engaging and making progress. Unfortunately, you can't assume that your child is participating just because the therapist hasn't mentioned otherwise. Some therapists may continue seeing your child even if there is no sign of progress. It's up to you to be proactive and make sure this therapist is genuinely helping your child rather than wasting valuable time and money.

What if Your Child Isn't Engaging in Therapy?

"The first step is making sure that there's consensus. The therapist and the family need to work together; therapy won't be effective without a team approach. Half of providing good therapy for school avoidance involves partnering with the parents. I like to make time for parent sessions, parent training, and child training, so the parents can understand what engagement looks like and use these strategies together at home. If your child isn't discussing anything related to their therapy or sharing insights, that's usually a sign of disengagement.

"If you're not seeing any development in terms of identifying and communicating their anxiety or possible obstacles to preventing them from going to school, that's another indicator. About three to five weeks into therapy, you should start seeing your child open up about these issues. If there's no progress in getting to school at some level, they are likely not engaging in therapy." —Dr. Daniel Villiers

Levels of Mental Healthcare, and Exploring Higher Levels of Care

As parents or caregivers, we are always searching for the right professionals and the right level of support and care to help our children. For some kids, there may be times when outpatient treatment is not enough, and the child would benefit from more hours of therapy and psychoeducation.

Our mental healthcare system has different levels of care to meet the current and changing needs of each child on their journey toward recovery. You might be familiar with the phrase "They need a higher level of care." This is often used by mental health professionals when they believe that the current level of care is insufficient to address a client's needs.

Assessing the Need for a Higher Level of Care

You may feel that your child needs a higher level of care, but you just aren't sure. Usually your instincts are right and you can solidify your decision by calling various programs that will be able to advise if they feel your child needs their program's level of care.

In addition, Rogers Behavioral Health, a well-known mental health services provider, does a great job explaining how to assess your child's needs, beginning with assessing the severity of their symptoms, and evaluating how much their mental health disorder may be interfering with their daily ability to function. If your child is having a hard time functioning or experiencing suicidal thoughts or ideations, they may need more intensive treatment.

The following is a brief overview of the levels of care that you may be considering as your child seeks mental healthcare.

OUTPATIENT

This is your basic once- or twice-a-week therapy session at your provider's office or online. Therapists must be licensed in your state to provide you with teletherapy. Outpatient treatment is usually the first level of care, where you start working with a therapist or psychiatrist. A therapy session is usually between forty-five and fifty minutes.

INTENSIVE OUTPATIENT (IOP)

IOP is the next level of care, providing many more hours of treatment. It usually involves four or five days of treatment per week and for several hours a day.

PARTIAL HOSPITALIZATION PROGRAM (PHP) AKA PARTIAL CARE PROGRAM (PCP)

Partial programs are a way to get intensive treatment without being in a residential setting or hospitalization. These are day programs where the hours of treatment are usually a full day, five days a week. Sometimes, partial programs are utilized as a "step down" program, when patients are coming out from an inpatient setting and gradually reducing the intensity and level of care. (https://rogersbh.org/about-us/newsroom/blog/guide-understanding-mental-health-levels-care)

Many of these programs have top-notch clinicians and therapeutic interventions specifically developed to help kids with school avoidance. Since school-avoidant children often avoid therapy, you want to ensure your program has strategies to help ease your child into attending. When you call these programs, you may first speak with an intake professional who will ask about your child's situation and explain their program to determine if they feel it is the right program for your child, and you'll have the chance to ask them questions to make sure you feel confident in this particular program.

ACUTE INPATIENT HOSPITALIZATION

This is the most intensive level of care for children in emergency situations. It is designed for children whose school avoidance, anxiety, depression, OCD, or other mental health issues have escalated into a crisis. These programs are usually within or affiliated with a general hospital containing a child's psychiatric unit or in a specific psychiatric clinic with a children's program.

The team treating your child will develop a care plan for their stay. According to a review of pediatric mental health hospitalizations at acute care hospitals in the US, the length of stay is approximately 4.7 days.

The purpose of this level of care is to stabilize the patient, help them through a crisis situation, and develop a plan for ongoing treatment upon discharge. The treatment plan will identify the next level of care needed, possibly including medication management, preferred modes of therapy, and referrals to other treatment providers.

You can admit your child directly, or they may be referred by an emergency room doctor, personal psychiatrist, psychologist, or pediatrician. These programs are required to have a school component, though it may only consist of an educational supervisor to assist with schoolwork provided by the child's home school district.

Before planning to go, you may wish to:

- Find out if a referral from a mental health provider is needed or if you can admit them as a parent or caregiver.
- Ensure the program is appropriate for your child by asking about the care team and the typical day.
- Confirm bed availability and inquire about any waitlist.
- Ask about the typical length of stay.
- Determine if they accept your health insurance and if they will submit your claims as an out-of-network provider on your behalf.

CHILDREN'S PSYCHIATRIC TREATMENT PROGRAM

These programs, also known as inpatient or residential treatment programs, cater to children in crisis without the immediate concern of self-harm or harm to others. Typically set in a homelike environment, children live together in dormlike rooms or houses on the property.

The length of stay is longer, ranging from thirty to ninety days or more. These programs offer in-depth treatment with specialized staff focused on first-line treatment for children with severe school avoidance, major depressive disorder, severe anxiety disorder, OCD, PTSD, or other mental health challenges.

In addition to intensive therapy, the programs provide a chance for children to step away from their everyday environment and focus on improving their mental health.

These programs generally include a well-structured school component. Here are some important considerations:

- **Insurance:** Check if the program accepts your health insurance or if they will submit your claims as an out-of-network provider on your behalf.
- **Referral Requirements:** Determine if a referral from a mental health provider is needed or if you can admit your child directly as a parent or caregiver.
- **Program Suitability:** Ensure the program is appropriate for your child by asking about the care team and the typical daily schedule.
- **Availability:** Confirm bed availability and inquire about any waitlist.
- **Length of Stay:** Ask about the typical length of stay for their program.

STATE AND COUNTY MOBILE CRISIS TEAMS (MOBILE CRISIS RESPONSE, MOBILE CRISIS UNITS)

Mobile crisis units provide in-person crisis stabilization services for people experiencing a mental health crisis. These mobile crisis units will come to your home to provide face-to-face assistance. Some programs are available 24/7, and some have designated mobile mental health crisis services for children. The services are designed to defuse an immediate crisis, keep children and their families safe, and intervene when you cannot get your child to leave the home for mental healthcare.

Federal guidelines state that nobody should be denied or delayed access to services based on their ability to pay; this is the standard practice of most mobile crisis teams.

THE EMERGENCY ROOM

If your child is in crisis and/or you fear they may be in danger, do not hesitate to go to your local emergency room. Some hospitals have a pediatric emergency room, and some ERs have a space for mental healthcare as well. So, if you think that an ER visit may be needed because your child is at risk of hurting themself or others, you may consider calling your local hospitals to determine the best one to go to.

THE 988 LIFELINE

The 988 Suicide & Crisis Lifeline has replaced calling 911 for mental health crisis and concerns. It is available 24/7 to call, text, or chat for access to trained crisis counselors who can help people experiencing suicidal thoughts or ideation, substance use, and/or mental health crisis, or any other kind of emotional distress. The 988 Lifeline is a direct connection to immediate support and resources for anyone in crisis. The SAMSHA (Substance Abuse and Mental Health Services Administration)

988 website stresses that this number can be used for a variety of mental healthcare supports, such as anxiety, depression, suicidal thoughts, concerns about sexual orientation, drug use, loneliness, trauma, and relationship worries: https://www.samhsa.gov/find-help/988/faqs#mobile-crisis-care.

Please do not be fearful about discussing higher levels of care as a possibility for your child. Also keep in mind that many programs will have a waitlist, so if you are even considering a residential program (RTC or inpatient), call programs for an intake now and get on the waitlist. You can always forgo your spot to another family waiting.

Final Thoughts on Therapy

As a parent who faced school avoidance for many years with my own child, and as someone who has heard from thousands of families over the years, I understand the doubts you may have had as you read through this chapter.

You might be thinking, *My child won't go to therapy. I won't be able to find a therapist who can help us. And even if my child does go to therapy, they're not going to engage.* This may be true right now, but it often changes over time. My son went through phases where he refused therapy, hid in the car, and wouldn't come out, but there were also times when he attended therapy regularly. Keep in mind that you can meet with a therapist yourself for support and assistance.

We know that finding a mental healthcare professional isn't always easy or possible. But don't lose heart. Even if you can't access a therapist, you can still help your child by working with the school to educate them on the subject of school avoidance, connecting with other families for support or advice, and potentially exploring alternative education options.

CHAPTER 3

Working with Your School

How to Get the Support Your Child Needs

Building a collaborative relationship with your school is essential to helping your child return to school. This chapter explains the resources schools have to help you and the laws that protect your child's right to an education, all through the lens of school avoidance. Research and real-life examples demonstrate that parent-school collaboration significantly improves the likelihood of a successful return to learning.

While this may sound simple—after all, parents want to help their children, and schools want to help their students and families—there are often barriers to effective collaboration. Fortunately, most of these obstacles are not deliberate; they simply stem from a lack of understanding about school avoidance.

Every school operates within its own ecosystem, shaping how it perceives, responds to, and intervenes with students who experience school avoidance. The level of understanding, support, and assistance your school offers often comes down to luck. It's not always as simple as whether a district is good or bad. Sometimes, all it takes is one kind and empathetic school staff member who wants to help you and your child. If you encounter challenges with your school, keep searching for a team member who can be your inside champion. That person might be a teacher, counselor, social worker, school psychologist, principal, or even the superintendent.

As you move through this book, you'll gain the knowledge and confidence to advocate for the support your child needs. While it may seem daunting at first, by the end of this chapter, you'll be empowered with the expertise and motivation you need to push for positive outcomes.

School Districts Vary in Their Responses

Each school district has its own culture and attitudes shaped by leadership, experience, and the strength of individual voices. Schools also vary in their responses because of

- **Unfamiliarity with school avoidance.** Many schools don't provide comprehensive professional development training in school avoidance, so staff may not recognize it or know how to respond appropriately and effectively, often confusing it with truancy.
- **Uncertainty about how to help.** Your school may want to help but not know how.
- **Challenges interpreting IDEA and Section 504.** We'll learn more about the **Individuals with Disabilities Education Act (IDEA) and Section 504** and how they apply to school avoidance in later

chapters. For now, just note that these laws weren't written with school avoidance in mind, which can lead to misinterpretations that prevent schools from using these resources to help.

- **Intentional noncompliance with IDEA and Section 504.** Some schools are overwhelmed and lack staff, and they may avoid the time-consuming process of providing evaluations and creating 504s and Individualized Education Plans (IEPs). Schools may also gamble on parents' lack of understanding about their child's right to a free and appropriate public education, as well as Section 504 and the Individuals with Disabilities Education Act (IDEA). They may assume most parents won't file complaints or hire a special education advocate or attorney. They might be hedging their bets that they won't be held accountable. While not all schools operate this way, some do.
- **Mistakenly assigning blame.** Even when schools understand school avoidance, many staff members can't imagine what it looks and feels like for a family experiencing school avoidance, unless they have lived through it themselves. They may mistakenly blame families, believing they aren't doing enough. They may not realize how difficult it is to get a school-avoidant child to attend therapy, or that even when children are in therapy, it may not be the right kind, and therefore not helpful.

Your initial experience seeking help will vary based on those factors. It's easy to feel judged and resentful if you're not getting the help you need. But don't be discouraged—schools have resources in place to help children access their education. When schools and families collaborate, the outcomes are always improved.

Engage the School Early On

Families facing the early signs of school avoidance often feel anxious and unsure because they don't know what is happening. It can be unsettling, and you may not know where to turn. As we discussed in Chapter 2, your first step might be consulting a mental health professional. But it's also important to inform your school early on so that they can get involved as soon as possible. Research and real-life feedback show that early intervention and collaboration between parents and schools improve outcomes. The sooner you seek help, the better the chances that your child can move beyond avoidance and return to the school building.

While verbal communication is fine initially, always follow up by putting your requests for assistance in writing. As soon as you seek help, start documenting your official communications with your school regarding your child's school avoidance. This helps keep the school accountable for responding within state-mandated timelines. Don't allow anyone in the school district to act as a roadblock to the services or support teams available. Early intervention is critical.

While verbal communication is fine initially, always follow up by putting your requests for assistance in writing.

First Steps

* As soon as you see signs of your child avoiding or missing school, notify the school.
* Make sure the school understands that you know where your child is, you're trying to get them to school, and you need their help.
* Don't adopt a wait-and-see attitude.
* Don't let anyone discourage you from seeking help immediately.

Navigating the school system to support a child struggling with school avoidance can feel overwhelming, especially when it's unfamiliar territory. Understanding who to contact and how to advocate for the right support is essential.

Who to Contact

In elementary school, it is straightforward. When your child has a problem, we inherently know to contact their teacher. At the secondary level of school, you may reach out to individual course teachers when your child needs help. But who do you contact when your child starts avoiding school and you can't get them out of bed?

Don't assume that your child's teachers and support staff are communicating with one another about your child's school avoidance. Schools often refer parents to a guidance counselor, but you can also reach out to the principal, the director of Special Services, or Pupil Personnel Services if you need further assistance.

It can be intimidating if this is your first time navigating the school system beyond everyday interactions with teachers and guidance counselors. Schools are organized like businesses, with different groups serving various functions, leaders, decision-makers, and a hierarchy of systems.

Your first thought may be: *How can they help me?* They are educators, not therapists or doctors. This is a natural question, as a lot of parents don't know the roles of different staff within the school. However, schools do have the capability to help, and according to education and disability laws, it is part of their job to identify students in need of help.

The support staff you work with may include guidance counselors, social workers, and school psychologists. Some schools have departments like Pupil Personnel Services or Student Support Services, and most have a Department of Special Education.

The number of support staff varies depending on the school district's size, location, and funding. For example, smaller rural districts may have only one or two social workers (or none), whereas larger districts like Cincinnati Public Schools or Atlanta Public Schools have over a hundred. The school handbook typically directs you to contact your child's guidance counselor after reaching out to their teacher. If more help is needed, the counselor should refer you to a school social worker or psychologist. But you don't have to wait for that referral—you can contact them directly.

School social workers often have more experience working with school-avoidant students than other staff members, as they are usually the first to get involved if the issue isn't resolved quickly. They often become case managers for school-avoidant students, and they can provide counseling and connect families with community and mental health resources. School psychologists specialize in assessing and addressing students' learning and mental health needs. They are the professionals who conduct psychological testing when you ask for your child to be evaluated for an Individualized Education Plan (IEP) and they can develop intervention strategies and provide counseling. Even if you are directed to contact someone else in the building first, school social workers and school psychologists are likely to empathize and understand the challenges of school avoidance. They are both good sources of information and assistance.

School Teams

There are usually several teams in a school that can help provide the proper assistance for your child:

- **School-based intervention team:** These teams may be referred to as Response to Intervention (RTI), Intervention and Referral Services (I&RS), Student Success Team, or Student Support Team (SST). Some schools have transitioned their response-to-intervention teams into Multitiered Systems of Support (MTSS).
- **Section 504 coordinator:** Under Section 504, all school districts that receive any federal funding must designate at least one employee to coordinate the district's compliance with Section 504. This is the person to whom you should submit your request in writing for an evaluation for a 504.

The following roles serve similar functions, but their specific duties vary depending on the school district:

- **Pupil Personnel Workers (PPWs):** Act as advocates for students and consultants to school staff and parents. They address attendance, discipline, counseling, residency, homelessness, and crisis support issues.

- **Student Support Services:** Provides specialized instructional support and resources to help students succeed academically, socially, and emotionally. This department typically includes professionals such as guidance counselors, social workers, school psychologists, and school nurses.
- **Special Education Department:** Works to meet the needs of students with disabilities by providing assessments and conducting psychological testing to help evaluate the need for special education, which can include counseling, educational, therapeutic, and other necessary services. This department ensures that students with disabilities receive appropriate support and accommodations. Schools may call their team of social workers and school psychologists the Child Study Team or the Student Support Team. This team is responsible for determining if your child qualifies for special education, which includes an Individualized Education Plan (IEP). If your child has a diagnosed disability (whether learning-, physical health–, or mental health–related), your first contact may be the 504 administrator (for a 504 plan) or the Child Study Team (for an IEP).

School-Based Intervention Teams (aka Response to Intervention [RTI] team; Multitiered System of Supports [MTSS] team)

Intervention is a targeted support and problem-solving mechanism to help students with academic or behavioral challenges. The intervention process involves a school team working to find solutions to help students succeed. The use of Response to Intervention (RTI) became widespread in U.S. education following its inclusion in the implementation of the Individuals with Disabilities Education Act of 2004 (IDEA), which allowed its use as an alternative for special education eligibility. Notably, it does not appear in the law itself, only in its implementation.

According to the MTSS Center (formerly the National Center on Response to Intervention), "A multitiered system of supports (MTSS) is a proactive and preventative framework that integrates data and instruction to maximize student achievement and support students' social, emotional, and behavioral needs from a strengths-based perspective."

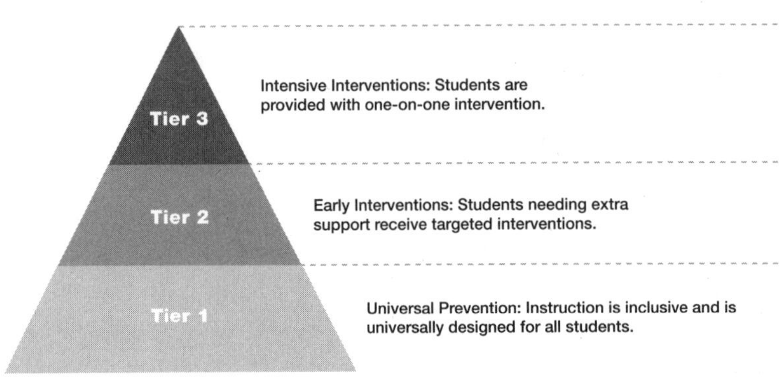

If you are unsure what this team is called in your school district, try searching online by entering your school district's name followed by "Intervention Team," "RTI," or "MTSS." This should lead you to the page describing this team's responsibilities. If you can't find information on the website, call your school to ask directly.

These teams are typically multidisciplinary and consist of administrators, the principal or assistant principal, school nurses, general curriculum teachers and/or special education teachers, and counselors.

If no one refers you to this intervention team, you should seek their assistance directly. You DO NOT need to be referred.

504s and IEP Evaluations

While working with the intervention team, you can also request an evaluation for a 504 plan or an Individualized Education Plan (IEP).

Some states, such as New York, Texas, and Florida, will require schools to use an RTI (MTSS) process before considering a special education evaluation. Be sure to check your state's Parental Rights and Procedural Safeguards Guide, which may also be called a Parent's Guide to Special Education (these guides are explained thoroughly in Chapter 4).

Meeting with the Intervention Team: Your First Opportunity to Get Help

Your first meeting with the school to discuss your child's absenteeism may be with the school counselor or principal (or the assistant principal if attendance issues are their responsibility). Schools vary in their procedures, so this could be a one-on-one meeting or involve an attendance team. Whether you initiated the meeting or were called in, your next step should be working with the intervention team.

However, the school may have you work with the principal or counselor for a while before introducing the intervention team. Since time is critical when dealing with school avoidance, ask to meet with the intervention team rather than relying solely on informal help from one staff member. The intervention team follows a formal process with rules, guidelines, and timelines, often outlined in your state's or district's guidebook, which can help hold the school accountable. It doesn't mean that they will necessarily follow these time frames, but it can help ensure that you are moving forward (especially if you live in a state that requires you to work with the intervention team before you can request an evaluation for a 504 or an IEP).

Ask in advance who will attend your meeting, whether it will be one-on-one or with the intervention team.

Preparing for the Meeting

To prepare for your meeting, gather the following information:

- Documentation or a diagnosis from mental health or learning professionals, including recommendations if available
- Details of any professionals you've worked with regarding your child's challenges
- Information about how your child's teachers have responded and what has worked
- A description of what is happening at home related to school avoidance (e.g., crying, hiding, refusing to get out of bed, or asking to be picked up during the school day)
- Steps you are taking to help your child
- Key insights from this book about school avoidance and its effective management
- Information on how your child is managing academically, socially, and emotionally
- A review of interventions that have already been tried
- Ideas for a structured plan with accountability measures (ensure that the intervention plan is written down, with a documented follow-up date to assess progress)

As you prepare for the meeting, remember to focus on building a collaborative relationship and emphasize to your school the necessity to intervene appropriately right away.

The Process Should Be Collaborative

While school professionals are experts in education, they may not be experts in school avoidance. You play a critical role in helping shape strategies for your child's success. During your meeting, share your knowledge of school avoidance and explain how the team can support your child's return to school. Remember that your input is essential to the success of the intervention strategies. Don't agree to anything that you are uncomfortable with.

Request an Agreed-Upon Follow-Up Date to Assess Progress

Ensure that a follow-up meeting is scheduled to determine if the intervention plan is working. A reasonable time to reassess should be four to eight weeks. Don't let this timeline slide—monitor your child's progress closely. If there's no improvement, contact the team to discuss additional strategies. If the plan isn't helping, or if this team lacks the experience needed, consider moving on to the 504 committee or Child Study Team (CST), depending on your child's specific needs. Remember, you do not have to wait for someone at the school to refer you to these teams. You have the right to request their assistance yourself—just be sure to get the request in writing!

Legislation to Hold School Teams Accountable

The following legislation, part of the Texas Education Code Sec. 26.001 (2019), was created to improve outcomes for students receiving intervention services. This serves as a great road map for holding school teams accountable to support students. Each state has its own RTI/ MTSS guide, so ensure that your school is following the guidelines. Schools should provide:

- A reasonable description of the assistance that may be provided to the child, including any intervention strategies that may be used
- Information collected regarding any interventions in the base tier of a multitiered system of supports that have previously been used with the child
- An estimate of the duration for which the assistance, including using intervention strategies, will be provided
- The estimated time frames within which a report on the child's progress with the assistance, including any intervention strategies used, will be provided to the parent
- Information about the parent's right to request, among other things, a special education evaluation at any time

RTI Should Not Delay Your Right to Request Evaluation for a 504 or an IEP

Susan Bruce, regional education coordinator for PRO-Parents of South Carolina, Inc., explains, "The RTI process *does not* replace the need for a comprehensive evaluation. School districts should not use RTI as an excuse to delay or, worse, avoid evaluating children suspected of having specific learning disabilities. Parents have the right to request an evaluation under the Individuals with Disabilities Education Act (IDEA) at any time."

Working with the Intervention Team While Waiting for 504 or IEP Team Responses

Even if you believe your child needs a 504 plan or an IEP, you can continue working with the school's intervention team while awaiting responses, evaluations, decisions, and implementations from the 504 or IEP team.

There is no law preventing schools from offering support via the intervention team while these processes are underway. Schools can implement accommodations through the intervention team without waiting for formal approval.

This is uncharted territory if this is your first experience with school avoidance—so give yourself grace as you learn to work with your school. Avoid the following common mistakes:

- Don't rely too long on one point of contact at your school if they are not effectively helping with your child's school avoidance.
- If the counselor isn't working on a solid plan, ask the principal to refer you to the intervention team (aka MTSS).
- If you find yourself constantly emailing teacher(s) about your child's attendance or academic problems, it's time to get others in the school involved.

CHAPTER 4

Educational Rights

Navigating Laws and Protections

At some point, someone may mention accommodations and modifications, 504 plans, or Individualized Education Plans (IEPs) as part of getting your child back to school. These are all essential tools for school-avoidance families and can play a crucial role in returning your child to their education.

We understand that laws like 504s and IEPs can be confusing, especially for school-avoidance families. It's easy to find information about those laws online, but harder to find explanations of them through the lens of school avoidance. This chapter provides clarity, as well as the understanding and tools you need to support your school-avoidant child. Many parents face similar frustrations when trying to navigate these systems, as schools sometimes struggle to interpret the laws correctly through the lens of school avoidance. By the end of this chapter, you'll have a clear understanding of what 504 plans and IEPs are, how they differ, and how they can be vital in helping your child return to school.

Learning Your Rights Is a Must for School-Avoidance Families

It's important to remember that every child in America is entitled to a free appropriate public education. The right to a "free, appropriate public education" is commonly referred to as FAPE (rhymes with CAPE). This is a fundamental right, and our federal and state governments have passed laws to ensure that schools uphold this right for all children, regardless of their disability.

Unfortunately, schools often fail to inform parents of their child's rights early on. Parents usually only learn of their child's right to a FAPE once they're already deep in crisis and therefore aren't able to seek school assistance at the first sign of problems. Learning your rights is crucial when dealing with school avoidance, as schools may not always interpret the laws correctly. Because school avoidance does not have a formal diagnosis in the *Diagnostic and Statistical Manual of Mental Disorders*, 5th Edition (DSM-5), schools may not always recognize it as a real disability. Even though it's often linked to mental health challenges or learning differences, the confusion surrounding school avoidance can make it difficult to access the necessary resources, like 504s and IEPs.

It's important to remember that every child in America is entitled to a free appropriate public education (FAPE).

Defining Terms

The term *special education* may initially evoke preconceived connotations, but it simply refers to specially designed instruction tailored to meet the unique needs of a child with a disability. This instruction can include many types of support and doesn't mean your child will be separated from general education or placed in different classrooms. Similarly, you might be thinking, *My child might have anxiety or depression, but they don't have a* disability. Under IDEA, mental health challenges are considered disabilities. The legal term used, unfortunately, is "emotional disturbance." This can be unsettling for parents to hear, but it's just antiquated language—some states have recognized the term as tone-deaf and have changed it to "emotional disorder."

IDEA and Section 504 Define Disability Differently

- **IDEA:** Under 300.8 (1), a child with a disability means a child evaluated in accordance with §§300.304 through 300.311 as having an intellectual disability, a hearing impairment (including deafness), a speech or language impairment, a visual impairment (including blindness), a serious emotional disturbance (referred to in this part as "emotional disturbance"), an orthopedic impairment, autism, traumatic brain injury, and other health impairment, a specific learning disability, deaf-blindness, or multiple disabilities, and who, by reason thereof, needs special education and related services.
- **Section 504:** This defines an individual with a disability as a person with a physical or mental impairment that substantially limits one or more major life activities.

Child Find is another important part of the Individuals with Disabilities Education Act (IDEA). Child Find is a federal law that requires schools to identify and evaluate any child they suspect may have a disability, even if the child is progressing academically from grade to grade.

Child Find ensures that schools make it their duty to watch out for our children. If they suspect any possible disability, they are to report to their Child Study Team and evaluate that child for special education services. Child Find applies to children aged three to twenty-one, including those in private school, homeschooled, or unhoused situations. You can request an evaluation for your child under this law.

When No Progress Is Being Made at the Intervention Level

If you have been working with the intervention team (I&RS, MTSS, RTI) and your child still isn't making progress, it's time to request an evaluation for a 504 or an IEP. One of the biggest mistakes families make is waiting too long at this stage—the stage where you've been working with the intervention team or possibly just your school counselor; they may have tried strategies or suggestions, and *nothing has changed!* Don't wait for the school's next move—ask for the evaluation if the interventions haven't helped.

It's important to note that it would be inconsistent with the IDEA evaluation requirements for a school to reject a referral and delay the provision of an initial evaluation on the basis that a child has not participated in a Response to Intervention (RTI) framework. This means that if your school hasn't tried any interventions or given assistance, it cannot use that as a reason to deny your requests for an evaluation. That would be like the school saying you can't do step 2 (requesting the evaluation for a 504 or an IEP) without trying step 1 first.

504 Plans vs IEPs

Section 504, governed by the Office of Civil Rights (OCR), explains your child's rights and qualifications for a 504 plan. The Individuals with Disabilities Education Act (IDEA) of 2004 outlines how a child qualifies for an Individualized Education Plan (IEP). The plans ensure that every child, regardless of their disability, can fully participate in their education.

If your child qualifies for both, educational advocates generally recommend seeking an IEP, as it provides more comprehensive support and gives you access to services such as counseling, a resource-study skills period, cooperative classes, and executive functioning coaching, all of which can be particularly helpful in getting your child back to school. Note that 504 plans do not come with these (or any) services.

Another good reason to seek an IEP is that the school is held accountable for following the IEP and ensuring that your student is making progress toward the goals outlined in it. If that progress isn't made and the school hasn't helped your child return to learning, you have the right to request an out-of-district placement at the school district's expense. This option can be costly for school districts, and it's something they typically try to avoid.

The process of seeking a 504 plan or IEP requires submitting a letter to your school, requesting an evaluation. Based on the information you provide, along with the school's own data, the school will determine if your child qualifies.

You will need to specifically request either a 504 plan or an IEP. You *should not* send a letter asking the school to decide which one your child qualifies for. When requesting one of these resources, use your knowledge of the applicable law to explain why your child qualifies and needs it to access their education.

Each school has a 504 coordinator, although not all school websites list this information. If your school's website doesn't, you can call the district office to find out. When requesting an IEP, direct your letter to the district's director of special education.

Steps to Seeking a 504 Plan or an IEP

- **Request confirmation of receipt.** If you're sending your request by email, ask for a receipt confirmation. To be extra careful, you can also drop off the request at your school or district office and get a stamped copy to show it was received. This will start the clock on the timeline your state mandates for processing these requests.
- **Provide documentation.** Include as much documentation as possible. If you've privately hired a mental health or learning expert who has diagnosed your child or made recommendations, make sure the 504 or IEP committees include this information in their evaluation.
- **Add personal notes.** Explain what is happening with your child and what you've already done to try to help them.
- **Request a school review.** The school will review your documentation and determine if your child qualifies for the 504 plan or IEP that you requested.
- **Request an evaluation timeline.** If the school agrees to evaluate your child, the evaluations must be scheduled, completed, and reported within the time frames mandated by your state's procedural safeguards for special education guide.

If the school denies the evaluation, they are required to give you a written explanation, including the resources they used to reach their decision. Make sure this is provided in writing, as the school's reasoning may not always align with the law.

For children with school avoidance, getting the evaluations done can sometimes be a stumbling block. School-avoidant kids often refuse to enter the school building to meet with the school professional who will be conducting the testing for their evaluations. When this happens, schools might claim they can't perform the evaluation unless the child comes to the school. *This isn't true.* Schools have alternatives. For example, they may conduct the evaluations at a local library or other neutral space.

Since the process of getting a 504 plan or an IEP can take time (usually a couple of months for an IEP), continue working with your school intervention team in the meantime. Request any changes or strategies you believe could help. Remember, schools can provide accommodations and modifications now, even without a 504 or an IEP (as discussed under RTI in Chapter 3). Early interventions improve outcomes, so if your school resists offering accommodations and modifications during this period, ask where that stance is noted in your state's procedural safeguards guide. *Don't give up.*

The following is a modified sample letter from Ohio Disability Rights Law and Policy Center, Inc., requesting an evaluation for an IEP. You modify the language to your preference. Before sending the letter, be sure to make a copy for your records.

Sample Letter from Parent/Guardian to School Requesting Evaluation for an IEP

Date (include month, day, and year)

Name of Special Education Director or Principal
Name of School
Street Address
City, State, Zip Code

Dear (Special Education Director or Principal):

I am writing to request that my child, (child's name), be evaluated for special education and related services. I am concerned that (child's name) is having problems with school avoidance (you can include if they have a diagnosed mental health disorder or learning disability or if you suspect they have a learning difference or mental health disorder) and they need special education services in order to access their education. (Child's name) is in the (number of grade) grade at (name of school). (Teacher's name) is their teacher.

Specifically, I am concerned because (child's name) (explain what your child does or does not do and give a few direct examples of your child's problems at school).

We have tried the following to help (child's name): (If you or the school have done anything extra to help your child, briefly state it here.)

This letter serves as my request and consent for an initial evaluation of my child. Please confirm receipt of this email (or letter) and provide me with the name and email or telephone number of the person who will be forwarded this letter and who will be coordinating the initial evaluation. You can reach me at (email address) or at (phone number).

Thank you for your prompt attention to my request. I look forward to hearing from you.

Sincerely,
Your Name
Street Address
City, State, Zip Code
Daytime telephone number

What Does the Section 504 Law Say, and Does My Child Qualify?

According to the Office of Civil Rights (OCR), to be protected under Section 504, a student must be determined to have a physical or mental impairment that substantially limits one or more major life activities; and have a record of such an impairment, or be regarded as having such an impairment.

The determination of whether a student has a physical or mental impairment that substantially limits a major life activity must be based on an individual inquiry. The Section 504 regulatory provision at 34 C.F.R. 104.3(j)2(I) defines a physical or mental impairment as any physiological disorder or condition, or any mental or psychological disorder, such as emotional or mental illness, and specific learning disabilities.

For a child with school avoidance, let's break down the two criteria:

1. "Have a physical or mental impairment that substantially limits one or more major life activities."

Children with school avoidance often have a mental health disorder and/or learning disability (or are suspected to have one), which qualifies as a mental impairment. That impairment substantially limits one or more major life activities.

Major life activities, as defined in the Section 504 regulations at 34 C.F.R. 104.3(j)(2)(ii), include:

* Caring for oneself
* Performing manual tasks
* Walking
* Seeing
* Hearing
* Speaking
* Breathing
* Learning
* Working
* Eating
* Sleeping
* Standing
* Lifting
* Bending
* Reading
* Concentrating
* Thinking
* Communicating

A child who has school avoidance may have a mental impairment that limits one or more major life activities, such as learning, thinking, reading, sleeping, communicating, or even caring for oneself (e.g., not showering or brushing their teeth). Since the list of major life activities is not exhaustive, going to school daily or socializing with other children can also be considered major life activities. Therefore, they meet the first criterion.

2. "Have a record of such an impairment, or be regarded as having such an impairment."

Your child likely has a record of absenteeism, not completing schoolwork, or a diagnosis from a mental health professional or learning specialist, which satisfies this second criterion.

If the school denies the evaluation, they are required to give you a written explanation, including the resources they used to reach their decision.

Important Points to Note

- The list of examples of major life activities under the Section 504 regulatory provision is "not exhaustive." This means any activity or function not specifically listed can still be considered a significant life activity if it substantially limits the individual.
- The determination of substantial limitation must be made on a case-by-case basis for each student, as required by Section 504 at 34 C.F.R. 104.35(c). A group of knowledgeable persons must draw on various sources to make this determination.
- According to the OCR, "School districts violate Section 504 when they deny or delay evaluating a student when it would have been reasonable for a staff member to suspect that the student has a disability and needs special education or related services because of that disability."
- The definition of disability under Section 504 is construed broadly, and the determination of whether an individual has a disability should not require "extensive analysis." Notably, Section 504 does not mention needing a medical or mental health

diagnosis to qualify. It simply requires the determination that a student has a physical or mental impairment that substantially limits one or more major life activities, or has a record of such an impairment, or is regarded as having such an impairment.

Another Key Aspect to Consider

Grades alone are insufficient for determining whether a student has a disability. They are not the sole factor in deciding whether a student with a disability needs special education or related services. Grades are just one consideration and do not reveal how much effort or how many outside resources were required for the student to achieve those grades. Too often, schools incorrectly use non-failing grades as an excuse to deny a student a 504 or an IEP. As Section 504 outlines, that is not a valid basis for denial.

Section 504 Evaluation Requirements

Before a child can receive a 504 plan, an evaluation is required to determine if they qualify. This evaluation is a data-gathering process and does not require formal testing like an IEP does. The information gathered must be from a variety of sources, such as:

- Parent notes explaining what is happening at home and in school, and what has been tried to help.
- Doctor's notes from a pediatrician or mental health professional, which may include a diagnosis, observations, or recommendations (if available).
- Test scores (the school will gather these).
- Observations by school staff or other professionals.

Decisions regarding who qualifies for Section 504 cannot rely solely on one data point, like a doctor's diagnosis or academic grades. Importantly, **a medical diagnosis is *not* required** to qualify under Section 504.

If you still have questions about Section 504, the OCR link, "Frequently Asked Questions About Section 504 and the Education of Children with Disabilities," provides helpful clarification and answers.

Importantly, a medical diagnosis is *not* required to qualify under Section 504.

How a 504 Plan Can Help a Child with School Avoidance

A 504 plan should include *both* accommodations and modifications that help your school-avoidant child access their education. These terms are often used interchangeably, but they are distinct:

- **Accommodations** help students access learning materials and complete coursework by removing barriers and providing extra assistance. For example, a student is allowed to take an exam in a quiet room free of distractions.
- **Modifications** change what students are taught or reduce the requirements of a task. An example is reducing the number of homework questions.

The law doesn't specify exactly what accommodations or modifications should be included in a 504 plan—that depends on the individual needs of the student and your input.

One critical modification for kids with school avoidance is adjusting attendance requirements. This is often a point of contention with schools, as responses can vary depending on the team's empathy and understanding. Although school leaders might say, "We can't change the attendance policy," accommodations *can* be made to help students access their education.

There are no restrictions regarding what supports might be appropriate under a 504 plan or an IEP. Accommodations and modifications should always be based on the child's specific needs. However, an IEP is required for related services like counseling, access to study skills (also known as the inclusion or resource room), or additional academic help. Temporary modifications to workload are essential for school-avoidant kids. They cannot be expected to return to school and immediately face a backlog of schoolwork, as that fear can be a significant barrier to re-engagement. Remember, you don't need a referral from a school staff member to request a 504 evaluation.

Individualized Education Plans (IEPs) under IDEA

IEPs include accommodations and modifications but differ from 504 plans as they also include services such as counseling, skills groups, training, and transportation, with federal funding covering these services.

The team responsible for IEPs may be called the **Student Support Team** or **Child Study Team**. The team reports to the director of special education and is typically composed of social workers and school psychologists. If your child qualifies for an IEP, a lead case worker, often a school social worker, will manage it.

Qualifications for an Individualized Education Plan (IEP)

For a student to qualify for an IEP:

1. They must be found to have one of the thirteen characteristics of disability (as listed below).
2. The disability must adversely affect their educational performance.
3. The child, by reason thereof, needs special education and related services.

If your child is unable to access their education due to school avoidance and has a diagnosed emotional regulation disorder (which means a mental health challenge, or any of the thirteen categories), and needs special education and related services, your school is required by law to help them access their education through an IEP, or pay for another school where your child can be educated (out-of-district placement). When schools refer to out-of-district placement, they may consider alternative schools, therapeutic schools, private schools, or public schools that have specialized support and services. Remember to get a copy of your state's guide to special education. State laws will sometimes vary from federal law, and they can also vary from state to state.

The Thirteen Categories of Disability in Special Education, as Defined by the Individuals with Disabilities Education Act (IDEA)

- Autism
- Deaf-blindness
- Deafness
- Emotional regulation impairment (mental health disorder)

- Hearing impairment
- Intellectual disability
- Orthopedic impairment
- Multiple disabilities
- Other health impairment
- Specific learning disability
- Speech or language impairment
- Traumatic brain injury
- Visual impairment (including blindness)

Many Kids with School Avoidance Qualify for an IEP

Many kids with school avoidance have mental health challenges, learning differences, or both. It makes sense that kids with school avoidance meet the criteria IDEA defines as an emotional regulation impairment (mental health challenge). IDEA defines an emotional regulation impairment that qualifies for special education as a condition exhibiting one or more of the following characteristics over a long period to a marked degree that *adversely affects* a child's educational performance:

- An inability to learn that cannot be explained by intellectual, sensory, or health factors
- An inability to build or maintain satisfactory interpersonal relationships with peers and teachers
- Inappropriate types of behavior or feelings under normal circumstances
- A general pervasive mood of unhappiness or depression
- A tendency to develop physical symptoms or fears associated with personal or school problems

Logic Tells Us

* If your child cannot attend school, they cannot get into a classroom environment, affecting their learning ability.
* If your child is not in school, they are not socializing with their peers or interacting with teachers, which probably affects their ability to build good interpersonal relationships with peers and teachers.
* Your child's inability to get to school or the crying/yelling/tantrums associated with fears of going to school are inappropriate behaviors or feelings under normal circumstances.
* If your child is scared and unable to attend school, they may have a pervasive mood of unhappiness or depression.
* Your child most likely has fears associated with this problem of not attending school and may have physical symptoms as well.

Diving into "Adversely Affects"

In the definition of disability according to IDEA, the condition must "adversely affect" educational performance. This does not mean a child has to have failing grades to receive special education to qualify for an IEP; rather, it means that the child is unable to access their education due to school avoidance and has a diagnosed emotional regulation disorder (or any of the thirteen characteristics). In that case, the school is required by law to help the child access their education through services in an IEP or pay for another school where they can be educated.

The Components of an IEP

You worked so hard to get your child's IEP and are relieved and happy when it is approved. You may have been focused on accommodations and modifications; that is what we keep reading about, and they are significant! But pay attention to the other components of the IEP. Many sections are imperative in ensuring that your school-avoidant child gets back to school. The IEP tracks the school's progress in helping your child and keeps the school accountable.

The Present Levels of Academic Achievement and Functional Performance (PLAAFP)

The PLAAFP describes how your child is doing right now. This includes their academic skills and abilities based on their evaluations, grades, teacher feedback, and information provided by you, the parent. Equally important is your child's present "functional" ability, which means routine activities of everyday living. Going to school is considered a regular activity for a child. School-avoidant children have problems attending school, so be sure to add school avoidance to this statement. You have every right to add this information to the IEP.

Annual goals are year-long measurable goals that the student can reasonably accomplish. They are broken down into objectives or benchmarks so the parents and school can monitor progress throughout the IEP.

If your child is school avoidant, ensure that returning to school is part of the annual goals. This can be for small amounts of time when working on reintegration back to school. If the school cannot help you meet these goals, then *they may* have to make an out-of-district placement to a school that can help your child access their education.

Services provided cover the special education services and related services your child can receive. Services can include but are not limited to:

- Counseling with a school counselor, social worker, school psychologist, or outside mental health provider.
- Enrollment in a cooperative classroom that has two teachers (one general education teacher and one special education teacher). These classes are beneficial because the special education teacher can give extra attention and help to your child. These classrooms are for all students, not just those who have IEPs. The students in these classrooms have no idea that the extra teacher is more than an assistant teacher. These teachers are usually the ones who will ensure that your child is getting all the accommodations and modifications in their IEP.
- Resource room (aka study skills, various names). This class usually replaces an elective or a study hall. These classes are generally appreciated and very helpful to students. A special education teacher runs this class, and their role is to help your child organize, understand, and complete their work from all their classes. These teachers will often communicate and coordinate with all your child's teachers to help your child keep up and get extra assistance if needed. (If they don't do this, you should ask for it.) Schools usually allow students to take tests in this classroom or finish tests there if they need extra time.
- Executive functioning (EF) skills training: EF skills are the abilities in our brain that help us complete everyday tasks. These skills include planning, organization, time management, metacognition, working memory, self-control, attention, flexibility, and perseverance.

- Social skills training: Social skills training for youth focuses on teaching and practicing essential interpersonal skills to help young people navigate social interactions more effectively. This training encompasses a variety of activities and techniques designed to enhance communication, empathy, problem-solving, and relationship-building.
- Transportation: This can mean that the school district provides busing or other means of transport (at no charge to the families) to help students get to their school or an out-of-district school for the school day or for other services.

Participation in a general education setting covers the time the student will be present in the general education classroom (as opposed to receiving special education services).

Testing information addresses how, where, and if the student will participate in state and district testing; for example, the student is allowed time and a half to finish the test, can complete or take the test in a different room, or can take the test with the special education teacher. Remember, your school team should also submit documentation for tests like the SAT and the ACT on your behalf to make these accommodations for your child.

The locations and times when special education services occur may, for school avoidance, include specifics about home instruction, if that is utilized. It should include any time your student is in a cooperative classroom (where there are two teachers; one is a general education teacher, and the other is a special education teacher) and if your child has a resource (inclusion, study skills) period built into their schedule.

Transition services begin when a child reaches fourteen years old. The IEP must include any courses the student should take to prepare for transitioning out of high school.

Progress measurement states how and how often progress toward the goals will be measured and reported. Remember that a parent can ask for an IEP meeting at any time (put the request in writing) to discuss progress or problems within the IEP.

Agreed-upon accommodations and modifications can be helpful for a school-avoidant child (see the list below for accommodations and modifications).

Parental Concerns

Parents have the right to include their concerns in the IEP process. These concerns can cover a range of issues, including:

- **Unidentified areas of need:** Parents can highlight areas they believe have not yet been recognized by the school, such as their child's school avoidance, and inquire about the school's plan to address it.
- **Home-related issues:** Parents may also point out challenges they see at home that may not be immediately apparent in the school environment but may impact their child's ability to engage or succeed in school.
- **Additional concerns:** Any other factors or challenges that parents are aware of, which may influence their child's experience and performance in the school setting, should also be noted.

Homebound instruction can be included in the IEP while school reintegration strategies are implemented. Regarding homebound tutoring, short-term goals and objectives should be specific and measurable. Remember, this is *not* a long-term solution. *Make sure the school understands* that homebound tutoring is meant to be temporary, as the longer your child is out of school, the more entrenched their avoidance can become.

Accommodations, Modifications, and Services for Helping School-Avoidant Children Get Back to School

For children with school avoidance, getting back to school feels **overwhelming**, full of fear and uncertainty. Not only have they missed school, but most have worries around social interactions and managing their mental health, and, of course, they have academic concerns. This is where appropriate **accommodations, modifications,** and services must be provided.

Attendance and Feeling Safe

- Ensure that there are flexible school start and end times, along with a flexible attendance schedule, which are critical for helping your child gradually return to school. This should be based on a **reintegration plan** grounded in exposure therapy (as discussed in Chapter 2).
- Allow the student to start the school day in a counselor's or social worker's office, or another location where they feel safe.
- Allow the student to leave class to go to the counselor's office or a designated quiet space (no questions asked). Many school-avoidant children report that just knowing this accommodation is available reduces their anxiety, even if they rarely use it.
- Ensure that the teacher or adult in the designated safe space does not rush the student to leave. **Check-ins** to ask if the student feels ready to return to class are appropriate, but avoid pushing them to go back too quickly, which may trigger more anxiety.

- Consider allowing your child to listen to music on earphones while they are in the designated safe space for added comfort.
- Designate a staff member with whom your child has a connection to meet regularly, helping establish trust and rapport. This person can serve as a "go-to" when your child needs support.

Schoolwork

- Reduce the amount of homework assigned during the reintegration process. Start with just getting your child back to school, and add academics gradually.
- Allow extra time for completion of assignments, especially when anxiety or mental health symptoms interfere with completion. These are called *extended deadlines*, but they should be realistic.
- Break assignments into manageable parts, with the teacher assigning one part at a time.
- Provide copies of teacher's notes to help students that have difficulties with note-taking due to learning disabilities like dyslexia, auditory processing issues, or attention challenges, allowing them to focus on understanding the material rather than struggling to write everything down during a lecture.
- Set limits for how much time should be spent on homework and communicate these expectations to parents.
- Consider eliminating homework altogether in the early stages if it has been a major trigger in the past.
- Allow class presentations to be done one-on-one with the teacher or through recorded videos.
- Use positive reinforcement and praise for work completed.

Tests

- Use alternative assessments to evaluate learning.
- Allow students to take tests over multiple periods or in different settings (e.g., study skills class).
- Provide breaks during tests.
- Offer multiple-choice or short-answer tests instead of essay tests if writing is difficult for students.
- Allow students to take tests in different parts of the classroom or in a quieter room.
- Allow extended time on quizzes, exams, and standardized tests (e.g., PSAT, SAT, ACT). The school should handle paperwork for accommodations with these organizations.
- Reduce the number of test questions as stated in the IEP.

Services

- Allow access to cooperative classes, which have both a general education and a special education teacher. The special education teacher can provide extra support as needed.
- Offer study skills or resource rooms where a special education teacher helps students with organization, understanding, and completing their classwork.
- Designate a special education teacher to help coordinate and manage your child's workload across all subjects.
- Offer home instruction (homebound) services, where a teacher comes to your home if your child cannot attend school. Hours vary by state, but typically range from five to fifteen hours per week.

- Arrange for counseling services, with the number of sessions and counselor noted in the IEP.
- Arrange transportation for out-of-district placements, if necessary.

Classroom Considerations

- Create a system where your child can signal the teacher if they need to leave without drawing attention to themselves (e.g., placing a red dot on their desk).
- Allow your child to sit in a preferred spot in the classroom.
- Permit early departure from class (three to five minutes) to avoid crowded hallways during class changes.

Get Your State's Parent's Guide

One essential but often overlooked resource is your state's Parental Rights and Procedural Safeguards Guide (sometimes referred to as a Parent's Guide to Special Education). This guide details the procedures and timelines the school must follow for IEPs and 504 plans. Each state's guide is available online, and printed versions are typically available upon request from your school district. Familiarizing yourself with this guide is an important first step in advocating for your child's education and understanding the laws that protect their rights. You can find your state's guide by searching online for "school avoidance alliance + get my state's guide."

Other Considerations

- If your child is not currently attending school, find a staff member who has a connection with them to try to build trust. This could involve meeting off-site at a neutral location like a library or coffee shop.
- If the school sends work home and your child completes any of it, ensure that the teacher acknowledges and praises the effort, even through a simple text or email.
- When your child is ready to return to school, make sure the first staff or teacher they interact with is someone they trust. Have a backup contact if that staff member is unavailable.

Challenges to Getting Support for School-Avoidant Children

- Many schools haven't received training on school avoidance and may mistake it for truancy. Staff might view your child's absences as a behavioral problem rather than understanding the underlying anxiety or mental health issues.
- Schools may claim they can't help if your child isn't physically present, but federal and state laws are in place to support children who cannot access their education due to disabilities. These laws protect children like yours, who qualify for modifications, accommodations, and services under a 504 plan or an IEP.
- Some schools may incorrectly interpret Section 504 and IDEA and deny your child's eligibility.

You are your child's best advocate. While schools might not fully understand school avoidance, your knowledge of your child and their needs will guide you toward the right support. Until schools receive comprehensive training on this issue, your role is crucial in advocating for what will help your child succeed.

CHAPTER 5

Legal Insights

Pressing Questions Answered by a Special Education Attorney

As a caregiver to a school-avoidant child, you may not have anticipated dealing with the legal aspects of educational and disability laws. However, understanding RTI, MTSS, Section 504, and IDEA, as outlined in previous chapters, empowers you to navigate the complexities of school avoidance with greater control and confidence.

When these laws were originally written, school avoidance wasn't specifically addressed, which has led to confusion for both school professionals and families when interpreting them. This challenge is compounded by issues surrounding attendance policies, compulsory education laws, truancy, and the proper identification of disabilities. Unfortunately, many schools lack clear protocols for addressing school avoidance, making it difficult to ensure that laws are properly followed.

When you feel that your school isn't upholding your child's rights, seeking the help of an educational advocate or special education attorney can provide clarity and support. These professionals specialize in the legalities surrounding education and disability, helping you to navigate the process effectively.

Educational advocates, also known as special education advocates, have extensive knowledge of special education laws. They can help clarify the laws and represent parents while working with the school district. They can be especially helpful when a parent feels emotional and doesn't want that to interfere with their child getting proper assistance. These professionals are not attorneys. As always, parents need to ask questions to ensure that they have the expertise and experience to help their children with school avoidance.

When you feel that your school isn't upholding your child's rights, seeking the help of an educational advocate or special education attorney can provide clarity and support.

Special Education Attorneys

A special education attorney, on the other hand, is a legal expert in state and federal education laws. If you're facing serious issues with your school district, such as a failure to provide a 504 plan, an IEP, or any component protecting your child's right to be educated, an attorney can offer peace of mind. Although this comes with a cost, many parents find it worthwhile when their child's needs are not being met by the school.

Now, let's address some common legal questions that school-avoidance families often encounter, with responses from an experienced special education attorney. Because this special education attorney represents school districts, I agreed to keep them anonymous so they could speak candidly without jeopardizing their relationships with their school clients.

Q: Can my school alter the attendance policy for my child?

A: Yes, they can. Modifying attendance policies is a standard approach to help reintegrate children with school avoidance back into school gradually. If enforcing a local policy would result in discrimination or prevent a student from receiving FAPE (free appropriate public education), the school must modify the policy. Even if a student doesn't need Section 504 services, the school must consider reasonable modifications to its policies, practices, or procedures (OCR Dear Colleague Letter, 58 IDELR 79, 2012).

Q: Can my child be retained in their current grade due to missed work?

A: Retention decisions are not strictly based on law, but on whether the child has mastered the subject matter. Advocates and attorneys typically work to prevent retention, arguing that missed work or attendance issues related to school avoidance shouldn't result in grade-level retention.

Where to Find Legal Representation

* Google educational advocates or special education attorneys in your area and ask qualifying questions to ensure that they are a good fit for your case.
* The Council of Parent Attorneys and Advocates (COPAA) may have listings of professionals in your area.
* Some states have nonprofit Education Law Centers (ELCs) that offer legal advocacy for educational rights and may represent families pro bono if your case meets their criteria.

Q: What should I do if the school tells me they can only help once my child enters the building?

A: That may be a breach of Child Find obligations. If your child is unable to access their education due to a suspected disability, the school should evaluate them regardless of whether they're physically in the building.

Q: Why would I request a 504 plan instead of an IEP for my child with school avoidance?

A: If your child has a qualifying disability under the thirteen categories defined by IDEA, they likely need special education services, which are available through an IEP, not a 504 plan. A 504 plan can provide accommodations but not services, and many school-avoidant children need special education services to support their return to school.

Special education services that may benefit a child with school avoidance include:

- **Study skills/resource room:** A small-group setting where students receive support with assignments and time management.
- **Cooperative classes:** Classes with both a general education teacher and a special education teacher, where the additional support is discreet but available as needed.

Q: What should I do if I've requested a 504 or an IEP, but nothing is happening?

A: You must put your request for an evaluation in writing, which starts the clock for the school's response. Most states have a ten- to fifteen-day timeline for responding to such requests. Deliver the request directly to your school district's office and obtain a time-stamped receipt.

Q: My school says my child doesn't qualify for a 504 or IEP because their grades are too good. How should I proceed?

A: Grades alone are not a determining factor for qualification under either Section 504 or IDEA. The school should look at multiple data points, not just grades, when determining eligibility. Refer to the Questions and Answers on the ADA Amendments Act of 2008 for clarification on this matter. It clearly explains that "[g]rades alone are an insufficient basis upon which to determine whether a student has a disability." For IDEA and IEPs, see CFR 300.101 FAPE. Each state must ensure that FAPE is available to any individual child with a disability who needs special education and related services, even if the child has not failed or been retained in a course or grade, and is advancing from grade to grade.

Q: What should families do if their school denies evaluating their child and they suspect a learning disability or mental health challenge?

A: If the school denies an evaluation, they are legally obligated to provide a written explanation of why they don't believe your child meets the criteria for evaluation. If they don't clearly explain in a written letter whether or not they will evaluate and instead try to offer vague alternatives, ask them if their answer to evaluating your child is YES or NO. Watch for this, as a school may try to avoid putting their reasons in writing, especially if their reasons for denying aren't legally sound. When a school refuses to evaluate your child, this can be a breach of Child Find.

If You Fear Upsetting Your School by Bringing in an Outside Advocate

Remember this process is about standing up for your child's rights, not about keeping the peace with school staff. Many school professionals are aware of the systemic challenges you face and may even feel relief that you've brought in additional support. Remember, you're ensuring that your child gets the help they need and deserve; you're not responsible for managing the school's feelings.

Q: I've been told not to let the school designate "emotional disturbance" on my child's IEP because it will follow them, and private schools may deny admission. Is this true?

A: This is a misconception. By federal law, your child's high school transcript *will not mention* whether they have a 504 plan or an IEP, nor will it indicate their disability designation. There is no evidence that private schools deny admission based on the ED designation.

Q: Who can I contact if my school team isn't providing the help I need?

A: Your first point of contact should be the director of special education. If this individual isn't helpful, you can escalate to their supervisor, who may be an assistant superintendent. In smaller districts, the superintendent may be the appropriate person to approach.

Q: My school evaluated my child months ago but keeps postponing our meeting. Is this allowed?

A: No, this is against the law. IDEA and state regulations include specific timelines to protect families from such delays.

Q: What are my options if no one in my school is helping and they are not following Child Find, Section 504, or IDEA?

A: If your school is violating these regulations and no one is willing to assist, you can file a complaint with your State Educational Agency (SEA) or seek help from an educational advocate or special education attorney. State Educational Agencies track special education complaints, so you can search to find other cases that may look like yours or to see if your school has been cited before. FYI: Your state's educational agency (SEA) is another term for your state's department of education. For example, in Massachusetts, it's called DESE (Department of Elementary and Secondary Education), and in Texas, it's called TEA (Texas Education Agency).

Filing a Complaint with Your SEA: Each state has procedures for investigating and resolving complaints related to IDEA violations. You can find your state's special education complaint form by searching online for your state's name and "special education complaint form." These forms are straightforward and simple to fill out. You must explain why you feel the school is not following IDEA and include any necessary documentation. The state webpages also include directions and information about the process, so you know what to expect from the investigation and determination of a decision. Your state has sixty days from receipt of the complaint to make a determination if there was a violation.

The school must adhere to the SEA's decision, and their decision is usually not subject to appeal. You can find an educational advocate or special education attorney to seek a resolution. According to the Council of Parent Attorneys and Advocates (COPAA): "A special education advocate (also known as an educational advocate—not to be confused with an educational consultant, which is completely different) supports parents in getting their children the special education resources they need. They are not attorneys and do not have a license to practice law. They provide their services according to the laws of their state. Advocates are often professionals with training in special education and advocacy."

There is no state certification for educational advocates, so just like any professional you seek out, ensure that they have relevant experience with school-avoidant cases and have had successful outcomes.

As a special education attorney, I feel that educational advocates are particularly effective due to their knowledge of IEPs and for ensuring that all the components of that plan use effective language regarding your child's present level of functioning, goals, and action items.

Q: I am nervous about filing a complaint because I fear my school might retaliate against my child or make this process harder for us. What should I do?

A: If you have proof that the school is working against you or your child intentionally, that could be significant evidence for a case involving monetary damages. Retaliation is illegal. Filing a complaint could also force the school to correct the violation, benefiting your child.

Q: My school says they can't evaluate my child because my child isn't physically in the school building for testing. What should we do?

A: This is false. Evaluations can be conducted in alternative locations, such as libraries, other community spaces, or even at home. This is not a valid reason to refuse evaluation. Seeking help from an attorney or filing a complaint with the SEA typically has a high success rate in these situations.

Q: Can we request support for our child while waiting for the IEP qualification process to finish?

A: Yes, the IEP process can take around three months, so requesting a 504 plan as a temporary solution or asking for support under RTI/MTSS in the meantime would be advisable.

Q: Should we ask for homebound instruction?

A: That is a personal decision, but it should only be a temporary measure. Homebound instruction is meant to keep your child current with their studies while they are out. Most states have requirements ranging from five to fifteen hours of instruction per week for homebound students. Homebound instruction is temporary education, typically provided in the form of tutoring, to students who cannot attend their public or nonpublic school because of physical, mental, or emotional illness or injury.

Q: I thought accommodations were written into my child's IEP, but I don't see them being implemented. When I asked the Child Study Team, they said it was up to each teacher's discretion. Is this true?

A: No, that is not correct. The IEP dictates the accommodations and modifications, and it is not up to individual teachers to decide whether to implement them. You should request an IEP meeting to address this issue and ensure that specific accommodations are being followed as outlined.

Q: Should IEPs include specific language to define modifications and accommodations?

A: Yes, it's essential for IEPs to include clear and specific language. For example, a modification like "Joe will have the number of problems on his math assignments reduced by 50 percent" should be clearly stated to ensure that teachers follow it consistently.

Q: What advice do you have for parents who are sent to truancy court?

A: If you and your child are sent to truancy court without having an IEP or 504 plan and your child shows signs of a disability, that could be a red flag indicating the district failed to meet its legal obligations under Child Find. Additionally, truancy courts often offer families resources and paid services, such as counseling.

Financial Considerations

Parents often grapple with the decision of reaching out to an educational advocate or special education attorney. If you feel you need one, you probably do, so try not to second-guess yourself. You may be reluctant to seek this additional help because you have no idea how to find it, you are concerned your school won't like that, or you are worried about the cost. Let's address these concerns.

Don't assume you can't afford these services—always call to find out costs. Often, the investment in an advocate or attorney will pay off in helping your child sooner rather than later, preventing things from worsening. You'll also save energy, stress, and worry by having an expert guide you through this complicated process.

CHAPTER 6

Daily Strategies

Routines for Mornings, Days at Home, and School Nights

For parents of school-avoidant children, every part of the day can feel like a minefield—school day mornings, the daytime when they are not in school, and nighttime in preparation for the next day of school. But the most anxiety-inducing time is, bar none, the morning of a school day. You are fraught with fear of the unknown and anticipatory anxiety.

You have no idea what you'll get when you walk into your child's bedroom to make sure they're up for school. Although parents have the most questions about handling their child's school avoidance in the morning, there is little guidance in books or online. This is partly because clinicians don't always agree on the best way to handle these situations. Let's break it down and hopefully give you some guidance on what might work best for you and your child.

Experts offer varied approaches to managing these routines, so find the response that best suits your needs. Here, we will hear from

- **Dr. Rebecca Sachs,** a clinical psychologist specializing in autism, OCD, anxiety, and school avoidance, and co-founder of *Successful School Transitions*, a practice dedicated to supporting families facing school avoidance challenges.
- **Dr. Erica Miller,** a New York and New Jersey state-licensed clinical psychologist, specializing in neuropsychological assessment and evidence-based treatments. She is the founder and director of Connected Minds NYC, and co-founder of *Successful School Transitions.* She also teaches as an adjunct associate professor at Teachers College, Columbia University.
- **Dr. Daniel Villiers,** co-founder of Mountain Valley Treatment Center and the Anxiety Institute (who we heard from in Chapter 1) also treats school refusal as a mental health issue, and has successfully treated school-avoidance clients with specific strategies for almost two decades. He offers family coaching to help parents get their children out the door and to school during challenging mornings. His work is based on evidence, research, and years of experience in private practice and a residential outpatient program for anxiety disorders.

Dr. Sachs observes that school-refusal behaviors indicate that there is an underlying, legitimate mental health issue that must be properly addressed: "Parents need to remember and relay to their kids: 'Yes, we believe in you. You have this mental health issue. We have confidence you can handle this. We may need to participate in medical interventions, which aren't necessarily fun or easy, but they will get us where we belong.'" Experts consistently agree that parents must align with their children as allies and partners in this journey, providing them with the help and support they need. It's best to approach the situation as a mental health issue that is preventing your child from going to school.

Experts consistently agree that parents must align with their children as allies and partners in this journey, providing them with the help and support they need.

Q: What should parents do when their child cries or screams in the morning because they don't want to go to school?

A: Dr. Sachs: When your child is kicking, screaming, and crying, you must wait it out, which is a big dilemma if you must go to work. Part of this behavior is the child's way of escaping or avoiding school due to discomfort and distress. We can't help our kids when they're in a fight-or-flight state. Let your child calm down and get back to baseline. This doesn't mean giving up on school. It means we let the child learn to cope and adapt.

A: Dr. Miller: We need to show belief in our children's ability to cope and allow them to work through things. We want to help our kids build skills, feel empowered, and become competent.

Q: Is your advice different for younger children?

A: Dr. Sachs: If we're talking about younger kids, parents wield more power and can take more decisive action. They may need to follow a special plan to get their child to school, making it clear that this is not optional. It's like treating an illness—you wouldn't let your child avoid going to the doctor or taking medication just because they don't want to. School is necessary, and getting there is not optional.

Q: One of the most common questions parents ask is "What do you do in the morning when they wake up and refuse school?"

A: Dr. Villiers: It's about establishing a radically new relationship with your child, who is dealing with a medical condition. You need to use a different language and approach that employs techniques from motivational interviewing, cognitive behavioral therapy, and acceptance and commitment therapy. It's different because it involves emotionally and behaviorally joining forces with your child against the mutual enemy; validating what the child needs to know and feel—that you, the parent, understand that the child feels helpless in their struggle.

The foundation of this approach is to emotionally and behaviorally join forces with your child against this shared challenge, using language and emotions they aren't accustomed to but desperately need. Your child has become fused with the condition, resulting in paralyzing fear, shame, and guilt.

The key is to validate what the child feels—acknowledging as a newly informed parent that you now understand how helpless they feel. They also need to know you feel the guilt (though you shouldn't) for not having known what you do now. This shift in perspective helps reduce resistance and creates a more supportive environment for change.

From your new role as emotional and strategic partner, the first thing I would say is "Your condition is pulling you to stay home. We need to listen to that. Based on how you feel right now, I think that's a good decision." Then follow it with something like "I want you to commit to *not* going to school right now, as we have to make decisions based on how we feel in the moment." What we also know is the anxiety you feel now is not a good predictor of how you'll feel in ten or twenty minutes. I refer to this approach as a paradoxical intervention, in that it presents a counterintuitive option—giving the child permission to avoid school temporarily—that defuses immediate resistance and fear. By allowing space for the child's emotions and acknowledging their anxiety without forcing action, it often helps the child regain a sense of control and, paradoxically, makes them more willing to engage in the very behavior they are avoiding.

You might explain that your child's anxiety may be at a 7 out of 10, which is high enough to stop them from leaving their room. Then, twenty minutes later, it might drop to a 6, and suddenly they feel like they can get in the car. But I'd remind them: *Don't let it fool you—it could spike again.* This approach acknowledges their feelings and helps them see that anxiety fluctuates.

To be clear, you're *not* saying, "I don't want you to go to school." Instead, you're saying, "I don't want you to commit to deciding right now. We're going to assess how you feel when we're at the school." You might even suggest, "We'll sit in the parking lot or a place nearby and see how you feel." A child might question whether you will follow through, and a way to respond might be "It is imperative that we have the freedom to escape and avoid intolerable anxiety in the moment, but I can't take away the opportunity to enter the school building based on the anxiety you might not have." The success of today will not be defined by whether you get into the school building or not, but by your willingness to try.

Q: What about the advice to make the mornings uncomfortable if they won't get out of bed—blast music, pull the covers off?

A: Dr. Villiers: I don't think that's effective at all. It's a simplistic strategy that usually just creates animosity. No, you don't want to make it comfortable, like serving them breakfast in bed, but you also don't want to alienate them. If you're blasting music, you're not really joining with them. They need to feel like you're going into battle together.

Q: What if they won't get out of the car at school?

A: Dr. Villiers: If your child refuses to get out of the car, adjust your expectations. Maybe today the goal is just getting to the parking lot. You need to make them feel like this is a victory. You don't define success solely by getting into the school building—it's too much pressure.

For your child, going to school might feel like going into battle. They already carry the weight of shame and guilt for not being able to attend. Understand and communicate to them that you know if they could get to school, then they would. It's vital for them to feel understood and supported in this.

You may also consider saying, "If we go home and not into school, I want you to feel good about it. I don't want you to go home and feel sad, frustrated, or disappointed. You don't deserve that. To prevent that, we just have to continue to commit to making calculated decisions in the moment, and if you are telling me that your anxiety is too high in this moment to get into school, we will go home and we can feel good about every decision we made together."

More often than not, a child will say, "I think I can go in." If they do, say, "Sounds good," and if they don't, say, "Sounds good," as the reality is any movement toward school is progress and what recovery looks like.

You could do this with any child. Amazingly, they get on board with it, and it's really moving. Remind yourself, "If my child could control it, they would!" Remind your child of this, too, as they will forget.

Q: What do you think about pulling a child out of the car and into the school building?

A: Dr. Villiers: That's like throwing a child into the deep end of a pool to teach them to swim—you'll lose their trust. You rob them of the opportunity to build their confidence gradually, like stepping into the shallow end and moving toward the deep end over time. Forcing them strips away the resilience they could develop through incremental growth.

If you're at the intervention point—in the car, and your child is refusing to get out—I'd suggest using a different tactic. Tell your child, "Right now, we're going to stay in this car until we assess where your anxiety is at in five minutes. Even if you're supposed to be at school already, it doesn't matter," and then reinforce that "we are in this together, and we are going to make decisions together based on how you feel in the present. That is all we can control."

You're siding with your child against their anxiety but also acknowledging the power anxiety holds over them.

Most kids have never heard language like this. They're probably thinking, *Wait, what? You're telling me not to do what I'm already saying I can't do?* It's a powerful, disorienting shift. This is the essence of paradox, a form of reverse psychology but grounded in love and logic.

Q: You discussed measuring anxiety in terms of a number. Can you explain that?

A: Dr. Villiers: I often ask children to rate their anxiety on a scale from 1 (lowest) to 10 (highest) to understand how intense their feelings are. Instead of directly asking, "What is your level of anxiety?" we say, "What is your number?" So, you didn't have to keep mentioning the word "anxiety."

A child who is struggling and whose anxieties impact what they want to do is usually okay with sharing their number. It is easy to share. It's also good data for the parent to know how their child is doing in the moment and how they are progressing over time.

Just as important, you should prepare your child by saying, "Your anxiety might go up to a five or six when you get to school; so expect that." Strangely, this tends to have a positive effect. Once they're prepared for the possibility, the chances of that expected outcome decrease. If it does increase, they are not surprised, and if it doesn't, they're pleasantly surprised. But telling your child, "Once you're inside, you'll be fine" is not helpful—it's better to be honest about what they might experience.

You can also set short goals, like saying, "Today, we'll commit to two hours at school and reassess after that." Most of the time, once they've been in school for two hours, they're fine and don't want to leave. It's the feeling of being trapped that heightens anxiety, so offering the option of escape can paradoxically make them feel less anxious. If you can escape, you're less likely to feel the need to escape.

Q: Won't giving them an "out" lead to more avoidance?

A: Dr. Villiers: If escape is part of the treatment plan, it can actually help. Allowing your child to leave the classroom for a few minutes, for example, isn't failure—it's meeting them where they are.

A lot of this struggle stems from the fact that the child feels they *should* be able to attend school because they've done it before. It's not unlike having a bad back—some days you can go running or play tennis, and other days you can't even get out of bed. What initially could be defined as paradoxical intervention will evolve into making decisions based on data. A rule of thumb is to meet them where they're at depending on how severe the school refusal has been. When a child hears that it's okay not to go, it can be a huge relief, and their mindset may shift. If they believe you recognize the emotional reality of their experience, they can join you in a different way. You'll be partners in this, and that's when gradual exposure work becomes possible. The essential part is for the child to know that the parent truly understands and that if the child could control it, they would—sometimes they can, sometimes they can't, and that's okay. The more you can approach it this way, the better the chance of getting your child out of bed and into school or facing whatever they are avoiding.

Q: Can parents be trained to use this approach effectively?

A: Dr. Villiers: Absolutely. That's what we do. About 10 percent of our clients start with just parent training, as we might not yet be able to work directly with the child. All kids are different, and there are situations where this might not be the right approach, but we can always tailor it as needed.

"Facing the fears that keep your child from school may feel like standing at the entrance of a dark, unknown cave, unsure of what lurks inside. The only way to overcome your child's fear is to venture into its depths together. The journey will be difficult, filled with moments of doubt and mornings of exhaustion, but imagine how good it will feel when you reach the other side—when the struggle no longer defines you, and you can look back and know that, together, you conquered what once seemed insurmountable."

— DR. DANIEL VILLIERS

Q: If your child doesn't attend school, should you interact with them as usual? Should you give them boring food or ignore them? (I've heard this advice a lot.)

A: Dr. Villiers: That wouldn't be my strategy. You might want to set some realistic expectations for the day, based on where they're at. These might be challenging for them, and they might not complete all of them, but they should have some achievable goals. For example, they could take the dog for a walk or complete an assignment. Each child's impairment is different, so you should have an individualized list of goals. It's important for them to have something to work toward, whether it's chores or academics.

If you're connecting with them, educating, motivating, and aligning with them against the condition, it will change the dynamic. Either they'll be in school or they'll at least be getting closer to that goal. If your child can do any schoolwork during school hours, that would be great, but there should be no punishment for not attending.

Always remember, if they could get to school, they would. You must approach it this way, even if you suspect manipulation—keep playing it as though it's genuine because it usually is. Of course, this depends on the situation, but the mindset of unconditional support remains crucial.

Q: What do you think about taking away devices?

A: Dr. Villiers: I advocate for gradual changes rather than taking devices away abruptly. You want to build trust, not heighten anxiety by removing their sense of security all at once. It's about creating structure, not punishment. If it feels like a punishment to them, it will conflict with your whole strategy of forming a strategic alliance.

Q: Should we talk about school the night before?

A: Dr. Villiers: Absolutely. You're in this together, and it's not something to avoid talking about. But frame it as a strategy discussion. Saying, "Are you going to school tomorrow?" is the wrong approach. Instead, "We will assess whether your symptoms will permit you to go to school." Celebrate the intention to go. Celebrate the intention to try. Embrace the wisdom of making a plan together and responding appropriately in real time.

Q: What about kids whose days and nights are reversed?

A: Dr. Villiers: About half of the students I work with have a nocturnal sleep schedule. It's totally flipped. Children may be up until two or three in the morning or later. Mostly, when it's related to anxiety, it's linked to self-sabotage. It's sort of a way to avoid getting better, a way to avoid having to face things that they fear. The fear of getting better and not being able to maintain that progress. Whether they are conscious of it or not, their coping method has evolved to finding safety in paralysis.

I remember this when I was a teen with school refusal. The nighttime was the only guilt- and shame-free time. I felt good at night. I could play video games, and no one was around. And then sleep during the day when I was meant to be at school. I think that's often how that evolves. And then you don't want to go to school, but now you've got a good excuse, you're exhausted. You're desperately searching for excuses. So, for me, and for most of the children I work with, a nocturnal sleep schedule is a symptom of an untreated anxiety disorder.

Using technology perpetuates it, so some boundaries need to be set at night. The only thing that certainly works is taking their phone away, turning off the Wi-Fi, and limiting access to technology. If they are staying up all night, it's going to make it a lot harder to get up. Controlling that part of it is very important.

Q: Do parental accommodations play into this?

A: Dr. Villiers: Definitely. When parents overly accommodate their child's avoidance, it can reinforce the belief that something is wrong with them. Anxiety is about perceived threats, and part of the treatment is facing those fears and realizing they're not real threats. A client once told me, "When my mom was doing a lot of things for me or rushing to protecting me, it made me feel like there was either something dangerous out there, or something deficient in me that I couldn't handle."

Q: Do you have any additional advice?

A: Dr. Villiers: Remember, while it's a mental health condition, if it helps, say it's a medical condition. The difference doesn't matter, as the impairment is the same. The goal is to reduce the shame, and language matters. This will help separate the person from the condition. Talk about it openly and have a strategy. Say something like "Let's wake up at seven and take it from there." But also acknowledge the condition—tell them you want to make the right decisions with them, knowing that this condition can skew their thoughts and opinions. Let them know you don't want to push them to go to school if they're not ready. This can be a great paradoxical intervention the night before: "If you're feeling really eager to go to school in the morning, let's hold off for a moment and think it through."

Also, I don't want parents to worry that they're pulling their child back by taking this approach. Often, kids are testing their parents, seeing if they'll remain unconditionally supportive and nonjudgmental. Prove to them you are and always will be.

Anxiety is about threats and resources. Part of the treatment is like going through a kind of hell, facing your worst fears and realizing the dragon doesn't exist. That makes you feel like you've defeated it, and then you feel amazing. When you come out, you want to share that accomplishment with everyone else. But you've got to go through some hell to get there.

Facing the fears that keep your child from school may feel like standing at the entrance of a dark, unknown cave, unsure of what lurks inside. The only way to overcome your child's fear is to venture into its depths together. The journey will be difficult, filled with moments of doubt and mornings of exhaustion, but imagine how good it will feel when you reach the other side—when the struggle no longer defines you, and you can look back and know that, together, you conquered what once seemed insurmountable.

What *not* to do

* Don't blast loud, annoying music or sounds to make it intolerable for the child to stay in their room. This is unkind and invalidates your child's mental health condition.
* Don't yell or say disparaging things out of frustration and stress.
* Don't threaten to call the police, the school, or anyone else. Don't threaten them at all. Remember: Your child needs your support, and you must project calm even if you're fuming or freaking out inside.
* Don't argue with your partner in front of your child if the two of you disagree on how to respond.

CHAPTER 7

Embracing Neurodiversity

Neuro-Affirming Strategies for Divergent Minds

As the years go by, I continue to learn more about school avoidance. Our community of families at the School Avoidance Alliance serves as a collaborative support system and a valuable source of information. I learn so much from families who generously share their experiences, and I am grateful to be part of this exchange. Over time, I've heard from more parents whose children with autism also experience school avoidance. Before this, I hadn't realized that children with autism are more susceptible to school avoidance, nor was I aware of the unique challenges they face.

In my effort to better understand how autism and, more broadly, neurodivergence can contribute to school avoidance, I sought guidance from three experts and a former student with autism. Their insights were invaluable, significantly shaping my understanding.

I'm excited to share this knowledge with you in this chapter and the next. We will learn from **Dr. Rebecca Sachs and Dr. Erica Miller**, who you were introduced to in Chapter 6.

Q: How do you define neurodiversity?

A: Dr. Sachs: Understanding neurodiversity is crucial when we are working with youth struggling to get to school. Neurodiversity is the idea that humans have naturally occurring variability in how their brains work and process information. When there are differences, they're natural and normal. Just like I am right-handed, and somebody is left-handed, some people are more concrete and literal in their thinking and others are more abstract thinkers. Neurodiversity acknowledges that these variations are natural and don't require fixing. When keeping in mind the idea of neurodiversity, especially in the context of how it applies to kids struggling to get to school, we are considering that the world is designed for the most common or the most typical. For neurodivergent individuals, people process information in a less common way; the world may not be designed for them. Similarly, school and how we do schooling are not necessarily designed for divergent thinkers.

It's important that we create a more inclusive and accommodating school environment. Part of that means we need to teach kids specific skills and support them in different ways, but it also means that we need to change what school looks like for them to make it a better match for neurodivergent youth.

A: Dr. Miller: No matter what, human variation happens across the board. We're becoming so much more aware that differences exist, thinking more about how we can support those, and talking about this in more spaces. And that is not a dichotomy of good or bad, including embracing the idea that learners are different, and need different tools and structures to be successful. Learning to accept those differences, for them to be appreciated by ourselves and others, though, is still very much a work in progress. Even though the conversations have begun, we still have a way to go.

Q: How is autism diagnosed?

A: Dr. Sachs: One important thing to remember is that there's no single indicator of autism, like "If a child doesn't do this, they don't have autism." I often hear people say, "They make great eye contact, so they can't be autistic." But difficulty with eye contact isn't a definitive sign. Autism is more of an information-processing condition, and while we know it's lifelong, how it shows up can vary widely.

Behavioral differences can appear within the first year of life, but some children, particularly those with higher IQs, stronger language skills, or greater social motivation, might not display the more classic signs of autism. These children may engage in prosocial behaviors, or even masking and social camouflage, which can hide some of the behavioral indicators.

There's a lot of variability in how autism presents, not only between individuals but also in how these behaviors change across different stages of life or contexts. Diagnosing autism through a more medical model, such as the DSM-5 (*Diagnostic and Statistical Manual*), requires looking at two main indicators: difficulties with social communication and social interaction, and repetitive or restricted thinking and behavior.

However, a neurodiverse-affirming approach would describe these traits not as deficits but simply as differences in how people process information.

Understanding Autistic Experiences: Thinking, Social, and Sensory Differences

General thinking differences

* A tendency to think in black and white or be more detail oriented.
* Difficulty with abstract concepts; thriving on more concrete and literal information.
* A preference for clear rules, predictability, and consistency. Sudden or unexpected changes can be particularly difficult.
* Challenges with executive functioning tasks, like planning, prioritizing, or initiating tasks. There's overlap here with ADHD, which shares some of these challenges.

Social processing differences

* It's a misconception that people with autism can't develop relationships, can't communicate meaningfully, or lack empathy. These abilities exist but may look different or take more effort to meet neurotypical expectations.
* Individuals with autism may struggle with the "hidden curriculum"—the unspoken neurotypical social rules and expectations that others pick up without being explicitly taught but are expected to be organically known and followed.
* Some people with autism develop a logical way of decoding social expectations, but doing so can be exhausting. They may mask their traits, hiding their differences to fit in socially.
* While some individuals with autism appear socially typical, they often express feeling drained, lacking energy, feeling they don't have the bandwidth, and needing recovery time after social interactions.

* Social situations that require spontaneous responses can be overwhelming, as there's less time to decode expectations.

Sensory processing differences: Where people may feel overwhelmed, underwhelmed, or both from sensory information

* People with autism may be overwhelmed by sensory stimuli like loud noises, strong smells, or bright lights.
* They might dislike certain textures in clothing or food or even be bothered by tags on clothing.
* They may seek a certain type of sensory input, like feeling textures of clothing or touching, rubbing, or squeezing objects, or find certain sounds soothing.
* They may seek sensory stimulation, like rocking, fidgeting, or moving their fingers.

Interoception (awareness of internal body states)

* This includes sensing temperature, hunger, or pain. Some people with autism struggle with modulating these signals. For instance, they may forget to eat until they're starving at the end of the day or may not notice the need to use the bathroom until it's too late. Parents or professionals may wonder, *Why didn't you think about it?* But in reality, it's really because the body and brain aren't communicating to each other in the typical way.
* Sensory-motor interoception is another challenge for many kids with school avoidance. Walking through crowded hallways or dealing with fluorescent lighting can be overwhelming experiences.

Q: Is there still a stigma attached to having autism?

A: Dr. Sachs: Even though we are making progress, unfortunately, there's still a stigma in society with disabilities as a whole. Sometimes even school professionals hesitate to share an autism diagnosis because they fear it will be received as bad news. However, getting an autism diagnosis can be empowering for many individuals. It helps them understand that they're not broken and gives them a framework for understanding how they process information and interact with the world. This, in turn, helps them know what to advocate for in terms of accommodations and support. It also allows them the opportunity to seek out and connect with other neurodivergent folks, to develop role models, as well as peer friendships.

It's important that professionals approach the autism diagnosis in a way that helps children understand that their brains work differently, not in a wrong or deficient way. Using a trauma-informed approach, we might say, "You've gone through something difficult because the world hasn't been set up to validate your experience." The more we ignore or downplay autism, the worse it can get. But helping children understand themselves can lead to better outcomes.

Having an autism classification can open doors to many services and accommodations, both through an Individualized Education Plan (IEP) in school and through health insurance. For parents, especially in the public school system, this label can be the key to unlocking the support their child needs to succeed.

Q: Can you explain the difference between using the term "autistic" versus "a person with autism"?

A: Dr. Sachs: There is a discussion in the disability community about what language is preferable. Person-first language is based on the idea that "I'm a person first, and then I have this disability or difference." So, I'm a "person with autism." Traditionally, in the special education world, many people were trained to use person-first language.

Alternatively, there is the idea of identity-first language. For some people, "I can't separate my autism from me. It is part of how I see and interact with the world." I have a colleague who explained it this way: "It's not like getting on an airplane and checking your luggage; I cannot check my autism. It's just baked into who I am." The preference for language is an acknowledgment that autism is part of one's identity. "I'm autistic."

Personally, I think it is best practice to discuss this with clients, students, friends, and children about the different types of language that exist and then investigate and use what they prefer.

Q: What is important for us to keep in mind about the emotional experience of autistic youth and its impact on school refusal?

A: Dr. Sachs: Many autistic individuals have the vocabulary to identify and then communicate with other people, but their emotional experience can be really challenging. Some people experience emotions like a dimmer switch, with subtle changes, but autistic individuals often experience emotions more like a three-way lightbulb: It's either off, on, or extremely on.

In terms of arousal, research into heart rate and the central nervous system shows that autistic people tend to wake up with a higher baseline arousal level than neurotypical people. This means that when something challenging happens—like remembering a forgotten assignment or having a difficult teacher—they aren't starting at a low level of stress. They might already be at a 4 or 5 on a scale of 10.

Autistic individuals often experience emotions with greater intensity or variability and struggle more with regulating those emotions. Studies have shown that both youth and adults with autism experience mental health conditions, like depression, anxiety, and OCD, at even higher rates than neurotypical individuals. This could be because the world around them isn't well-matched to their needs, leading to higher stress levels and making them more prone to mental health challenges.

While autism itself isn't a mental health issue, I believe that "autistic burnout" is. Depression co-occurs and is exacerbated because of being an autistic person in a neurotypical world. Also, anxiety and all these things are stand-alone mental health issues, which are complicated and exacerbated by autism or a learning issue.

Q: What are therapeutic approaches and strategies to help school-avoidant children who are autistic?

A: Dr. Sachs: There are a few key settings that are extremely important for autistic children:

- **Sensory-safe spaces:** Right off the bat—are they going to be overwhelmed sensory-wise? Is it a sensory-safe space? How can we make school, getting to and from school and homework, as sensory-safe as possible?
- **Functional communication:** Autistic children often have language-based challenges, especially when overwhelmed. Even those with high IQs can struggle to express their needs when they're emotionally or sensory overwhelmed. We need to make sure they have functional ways to communicate. It may even be hard for them to raise their hands and say, "I need a pass to leave the classroom," if they are

feeling overwhelmed. For example, some students may struggle to ask for a pass to the guidance office when they're overwhelmed. A simple solution might be an index card with a stoplight on it: When the student feels overwhelmed, they can point to the red part of the stoplight, and the teacher knows they need support.

A: Dr. Miller: Validation is also crucial, especially for older kids. Many autistic children feel misunderstood, and this lack of validation can contribute to anxiety and depression. They need neuro-affirming environments where they feel seen and understood. Without this, they can develop a negative self-concept, which can snowball into larger emotional challenges.

Q: Are there other accommodations or modifications schools should be aware of for a child who has autism and school avoidance?

A: Dr. Sachs: We must collaborate with the school and child to get a full picture of what this child needs and where demands can be reduced or eliminated. For instance, maybe it's too loud or crowded for them to enter the school building with everyone else, so they could arrive early or leave classes five minutes before the bell.

Some accommodations that may be helpful:

- Have a safe person and place where the child can go when they're dysregulated.
- Ensure they don't have to verbally ask for permission to leave when they're overwhelmed; give them a way to leave the room without needing to speak.
- Have a plan in place, like going to the guidance office, so they know where to go when they're feeling dysregulated.

- Provide executive functioning support, like a daily or weekly check-in to help the student organize their workload and follow up.
- Be aware that even kids who can speak well might benefit from an Augmentative and Alternative Communication (AAC) device to support communication when they're overwhelmed.
- Consider practical accommodations, like an elevator pass, if they struggle with navigating large school buildings.
- Provide food breaks if necessary, allowing them to eat in class when needed.

Even a student who seems to be doing fine academically can benefit from some of those strategies because they reduce their sensory load, which gives them more bandwidth. We have to take a broader view; it is more than how someone is performing academically that contributes to school avoidance.

At the same time, we need to be careful not to make the child feel more disabled than they are. The goal is gradual exposure to build resilience without overwhelming them.

A: Dr. Miller: It's so important to assess what adds stress to their nervous system, how various factors—sensory overload, social-emotional challenges, and executive functioning struggles—affect the child's experience. Reducing demands and personalizing their accommodations make them more available for learning, but also for their overall sense of well-being. For instance, if the child has motor difficulties, like dysgraphia or slow processing speed, they might benefit from a keyboard, keyboarding lessons, or the opportunity to record lectures. Even students who appear to be doing fine academically may need these supports to reduce their load and create more bandwidth for emotional regulation.

Q: When do you know that the school isn't the right fit and you need to consider an alternative placement?

A: Dr. Sachs: Especially for an autistic or ADHD kid, if the school isn't sensory safe, or doesn't at least have a sensory space where students can take a break and reset, we might want to consider alternatives.

I would advise parents to be aware that when their child becomes dysregulated, they might be placed in what is known as a "cool down" or "time-out" room. The function of these rooms can vary significantly depending on the school.

In some schools, these rooms are designed as supportive spaces where the child is not left alone and is provided with tools and support to help them regulate and "cool down." However, if these rooms are used as seclusion rooms or if the school has a policy of restraint, and you have concerns about this, it is worth reconsidering if this school environment is suitable for an autistic child or a child with a developmental disability.

CHAPTER 8

Autism and School Avoidance

A Parent Coach and Her Child Share Their Journey

To continue learning how to best support neurodiverse children who have school avoidance, from both the parent and child perspective, I sat down with Penny Williams, a parenting coach for neurodiverse families, and her daughter, Willow, who struggled with both school avoidance and autism.

Penny Williams is a parenting coach for neurodiverse families who teaches parents how to reduce chaos and maximize success for their neurodivergent kids. Penny is an award-winning author, host of the *Beautifully Complex* podcast, and creator of the Survival to Success Accelerator™, a parent training program designed to help parents celebrate and support their kids with ADHD or autism.

Willow Williams is a twenty-one-year-old high school graduate with autism who experienced school avoidance. Willow, an autism advocate, is exploring various career opportunities, including musician, puppeteer, voice actor, nurse, elder carer, and construction worker. She lives in Asheville, North Carolina, with her parents and two dogs. Her insights have greatly influenced my understanding of autism and neurodiversity, and I'm eager to share her advice.

Here's my conversation with Penny and Willow.

Q: Can you describe what it feels like to be dysregulated?

A: Penny: Dysregulation is when you don't feel settled or safe; everything feels out of whack. In contrast, when you're regulated, you feel calm and secure.

A: Willow: My dysregulation feels like panic!

A: Penny: I didn't even know there was something like regulation or dysregulation until five or six years ago. I had no idea during most of Willow's childhood, but it really is the key to everything.

Q: Willow, what does panic feel like?

A: Willow: There was a time in middle school when I was very dysregulated and panicked. I got dropped off at school, and ten seconds after leaving the car, I started running back after it. Sometimes, I had an explanation for why I felt like I had to run. Sometimes, it was just an irrational fear of something that I thought *might* happen. Other times, it was just irrational panic.

Q: What were your fears? And is there a difference between when you realize what's bothering you versus when you're so panicked that you can't think clearly?

A: Willow: When I was chasing after the car, it started with a minor panic I didn't even notice on the way to school. But once we got there, it escalated fast, and suddenly, I just couldn't be there anymore.

A: Penny: Yeah, you seemed fine in the car the whole way. You even smiled and said, "Bye, Mom," when you got out. Then I started pulling away, and I heard this bloodcurdling scream like someone had been hit by a car. I looked in my rearview mirror and saw you running into traffic, chasing after the car. Now, I understand that it was your nervous system reacting, whether you could identify the fear or not. Your body was acting to protect you, and it ran straight toward Mom.

There was another time you tried opening the car door in the middle of a five-lane intersection because you didn't want to go to school. You'd sit behind me in the car and punch and kick the back of the seat out of pure desperation—that's so unlike you. You're usually the most caring, empathetic kid, but that was how desperate you were.

Q: Willow, were you able to recognize what you were afraid of? Can you explain what might have been causing your fear at school?

A: Willow: There's the obvious stuff, like the fear of rejection or not doing well in front of your peers. But then there's also paranoia—seeing bad things on the news happening at schools and being a naturally paranoid person makes those fears stick with you.

A: Penny: Sometimes, I would sit and ask, "Okay, what's bothering you? What's making you feel unsafe at school?" In middle school, for example, you didn't want to change into gym clothes with the other kids, so you didn't. But then the teacher started failing you. It turned out the locker room was too loud and too scary.

A: Willow: Yeah, I didn't want to change in front of other people either. I don't know why they think kids should be comfortable enough to strip in front of others and put on a uniform. If I'm participating in PE, it shouldn't matter what I wear.

A: Penny: So we made a plan. I talked to the PE teacher, and they gave Willow a private bathroom to change in, which worked. Sometimes, the anxiety was tied to concrete things like that.

Q: What other things made you feel unsafe?

A: Willow: Pep rallies. My mom got me special accommodation, so I didn't have to go because they were so loud.

A: Penny: Even then, you still wouldn't trust that, and you still wouldn't go to school on pep rally days. You thought it was unfair that the teachers made you do worksheets while the other kids got a free period. So, we talked with the school staff and they agreed you could skip the pep rallies *and* the schoolwork. After that, you felt comfortable going to school on those days.

Q: How long did it take for the school to understand and listen to you?

A: Penny: Forever. They just don't understand sensory stuff or neurodivergence.

Q: Why do you think that is?

A: Penny: Because their system doesn't incorporate it. You can become a teacher without learning anything about learning disabilities, ADHD, autism, sensory issues, or executive functioning.

Q: Let's talk about sensory issues. What makes you feel uncomfortable or unsafe?

A: Willow: Loud noises and people talking during class, especially when we were supposed to focus.

Q: Isn't school always loud, though? Bells, teachers, students?

A: Willow: For me, it was more about the school being crowded than loud.

A: Penny: I think you felt the least safe in high school between classes, walking through the hallways.

A: Willow: Right, because there aren't any teachers around in the halls. Suppose a kid wanted to come up to me and hit me in the face. Barely anything could be done about it, which was more of a physical safety thing.

Q: Did you have a reason to be fearful of someone hurting you? What happened that made you think someone would punch you?

A: Willow: I was bullied really badly in third grade.

Q: I'm so sorry. And what did the school do about it, or did they do nothing?

A: Penny: Not much. The worst part was that the classroom teacher told me that the other kids in that family did a lot of rough play at home, so that was why. So basically, she excused it. Then Willow had a substitute, and the substitute said something stupid like it was Willow's fault. I called the principal, and luckily, she was amazing. She totally got it and never let that sub come back to the school.

Q: The principal sounds like an ally. Do you feel having an ally is really helpful?

A: Penny: Yes, but you don't always have one. I teach parents to find an adult ally at school and introduce their child to that person before school starts. I tell the child, "This is your person. They get it. You can go to them, and you won't be in trouble—they will hear you out." Otherwise, kids don't feel safe if they think no one understands or will listen.

Q: Is it hard to find an ally? How do you advise parents to find the right person?

A: Penny: It can be challenging. I had conversations with the principal in elementary school, and that helped. Then, Willow had one meltdown in fourth grade, and they referred her for a functional behavioral analysis (FBA) with a behavior specialist. That specialist was a huge ally. She'd talk to me before and after meetings, saying things like "This isn't okay, and I'm working hard to help you." I'd email her for advice, and she even got Willow an autism specialist from the county.

In another school, we had a principal who was an ally. If things weren't going well, I'd ask her to come to meetings. But it did create some animosity with other teachers because it felt like I didn't trust them. Still, when no one listened to me, I had to escalate things.

It's a hierarchy of people responsible for what's happening to that child in the classroom. The principal is responsible for the implementation of accommodations and the IEP in their school. To some degree, they're responsible for their teachers' actions. And then, if that didn't go well, the next step was the special education director for our school system. I went there a few times, too.

Q: What kinds of modifications or accommodations did you request?

A: Penny: Part of the struggle was that Willow is gifted. She's highly intelligent and verbally fluent, but writing, organization, and output are hard for her. Schools tend to judge you on how smart you are, and they think, *If you're that smart, everything should be easy.*

A: Willow: Reduced assignments were one of the most helpful accommodations. I had a physics teacher in my last year of high school who was awesome and accommodated that.

A: Penny: The guidance counselor also let her come in, sit, and talk instead of having to go to class and pretend everything was fine. Allies like that are great, but some kids struggle so much, and it's terrifying. Without other explanations, kids often blame themselves.

Q: Have you ever had problems with teachers not implementing the IEP? What would you suggest parents do in that situation?

A: Penny: We had one teacher who flat-out said, "I'm not doing those accommodations. I don't believe in them," even though she was in meetings with her boss and the behavior specialist. That shouldn't happen. You shouldn't have to ask every teacher for permission to implement an IEP. If I were in that situation again, I'd sit down with the principal and whoever's in charge of the IEP and say, "This is how I understand the law. What's in the IEP goes." If that doesn't work, the next step is to file a complaint.

Q: Did you file complaints?

A: Penny: Yes, with one school. They weren't following the law, and Willow ended up hurting herself because of the stress. I gathered all the paperwork and sent it to the state. The school had to undergo special education training and had a month to do it. Hopefully, that made a lasting difference.

Q: How long did it take to get a response from the state?

A: Penny: About a month. We first got a letter acknowledging they'd received the complaint. Then, the school had thirty days to respond, and after that, we got the final decision in the mail.

Q: Willow, what did the school do to make you feel comfortable being there?

A: Willow: In high school, I could go to a separate classroom to do my work.

Q: Was it a designated classroom?

A: Penny: It was actually the school counselor's office. They had sofas there, and Willow was allowed to go in and work. But it took years to get that. Initially, they'd send her to the nurse, but every five minutes, the nurse would ask, "Are you ready to go back to class?" which would just escalate things. Eventually, I had to come to pick her up. One day, after being home for an hour, she felt better, totally regulated, and wanted to go back.

The front desk staff wasn't happy when I signed her back in after thirty or forty minutes. They didn't understand the personal reasons for it. We finally got it into the IEP that no one should talk to her when she needed that space. That made a huge difference, and after we put that in place, she only needed to use it three times.

Q: Willow, what did you do in the counselor's office to settle yourself?

A: Willow: I had headphones and listened to music. Music helps me regulate.

Q: Can you explain the first time Willow started avoiding school? What grade was it, and what did it look like?

A: Penny: Fourth grade, when she ran into traffic trying to run away from school. That was the first time it ever happened. It wasn't as chronic as what some families go through, where kids are out of school for months, but it still felt emergent and stressful at the time.

Q: Willow, you're such a strong, resilient person. Getting yourself back into the building after all of that is amazing. It doesn't always happen like that for everyone. Is there something that gave you the strength to face the anxiety and go back?

A: Willow: I wanted to be successful. There were probably times when I thought, *Maybe I should just drop out because I don't feel like I can do this.* But I didn't, and now I have a high school diploma!

Q: Do you have any advice for families with kids who are out of school for a long time—days, even weeks—because they're scared or avoiding something?

A: Willow: It depends on what's scaring them. But I found that knowing I wasn't the only one going through these struggles helped a lot. Sometimes just sitting with another neurodivergent person who has been through similar struggles is more powerful than talking to a neurotypical person who says, "You can do this." My mom arranged a meeting with another kid who was avoiding school. We didn't even talk about school avoidance, just talked about other stuff. But the next day, he went back to school.

A: Penny: If every kid felt seen, heard, understood, and valued, they'd probably all go to school willingly. But we don't always make kids feel that way, and that's part of the struggle.

Q: Is there anything schools could do to help neurodivergent students connect with others?

A: **Willow:** They could create clubs for neurodivergent kids. There are certain interests, like chess, video games, or anime, where you find more neurodivergent kids. If a school leader who understands neurodivergence runs these clubs, it could help foster connections.

A: **Penny:** She had no idea that other kids felt the same way she did, which could've changed so much.

A: **Willow:** I had really bad social anxiety as a teen, but I was scared of getting in trouble, so I went to school and did what I was supposed to do. I was sick to my stomach all day, but I did it. It would have helped to know other kids had similar struggles. I just thought I was weird or broken.

Q: Did you ever experience anxiety or depression where you had to go to therapy?

A: **Willow:** Yes, but it wasn't for school avoidance. I went to therapy for a long time, but as a teenager, I didn't understand that therapy takes time to work. If I had the perspective I have now, I would have stuck with it longer. Back then, I wanted to feel better immediately. When that didn't happen after a year, I quit.

Q: If a parent thinks their child might have autism, what do you suggest as their first step with the school or getting evaluations?

A: **Penny:** A neuropsychological educational evaluation is ideal, though not everyone has access to that. It gives you a lot of information about what the child needs and is struggling with and offers recommendations.

Q: So, did you do that?

A: Penny: No, we did things in stages. First, we got an ADHD diagnosis through a developmental pediatrician. Later, we addressed dysgraphia (not a diagnosis, but professionally identified), as well as executive functioning. As we started peeling the layers back, we realized there was more to assess and figure out. By age ten, I suspected autism because social issues weren't improving like they should have if it was just ADHD. It took three clinicians to finally diagnose her with high-functioning autism. One clinician even told me at first, "I don't see it." But after testing, she admitted it had been hiding in plain sight. So that was the full neuropsychological evaluation. A diagnosis opens doors, but you can also help someone without one. You can work on their struggles and use their strengths, even without a label.

Q: Willow, was there someone at school who made you feel safe?

A: Willow: Yes, my special ed teacher in high school.

Q: What made this teacher special?

A: Willow: He was more like a friend. He was super chill, relaxed, and understanding. He was good at connecting with kids by being interested in whatever we were into.

Q: Did you see him every day?

A: Penny: Twice a week.

A: Willow: Another teacher let me listen to music while working alone, which helped a lot.

Q: Did this special ed teacher help manage your schoolwork and communicate with your other teachers?

A: Penny: Yes, he led the IEP meetings and was our main contact. Willow could leave class to go to his classroom if she needed a quiet place. She also liked talking to him in the hall between classes. She enjoyed being around him.

Q: Do either of you have advice for families whose kids have trouble connecting with other students at school?

A: Penny: Being social can be really anxiety-provoking for some kids. It's scary, and they often internalize it, thinking it's their fault, like there's something wrong with them. Without any other explanation, they blame themselves.

Q: Was it helpful to have an adult at school who cared about you?

A: Willow: Definitely. Just having any connection can make you feel safe.

Q: If you couldn't attend school for a week, how would you feel about teachers texting you?

A: Willow: No, no.

Q: What if they're texting you just to check in and not about schoolwork?

A: Willow: It has to be the right person. I wouldn't want my teachers texting me when I'm not at school to say, "Hey, how are you doing?" That would feel weird, and I'd feel pressured. If your kid doesn't want to go to school, don't pressure them about it. That's the biggest thing. Pressuring will only make it worse.

Q: So what should parents do?

A: Penny: It's tough as a parent. I was freaking out, and they never even threatened truancy with us, so I can't imagine how much stress other families are under. There's so much pressure. You still get those automated letters in the mail about missing days. We had a rule that if you didn't go to school, you couldn't play video games.

Q: Did you stick to that rule?

A: Penny: Yes, but it didn't help. It made no difference because none of that was the issue. I could threaten to take video games away for a month, and she didn't care. That's when you realize it's not a "won't," it's a "can't." Parents often ask me, "Don't you have to punish them or set consequences?" But punishing won't fix what's actually going on. It just makes things worse. In high school, she told me, "The more you pressure me, the harder everything feels." I wish I had trusted her sooner and backed off.

Q: You tell parents to model a sense of calm, which is so important but also hard to do. What advice do you give parents on regulating themselves when their child isn't attending school?

A: Penny: You take a deep breath and accept that pressure won't change anything. You have to get to a point where you understand that forcing the issue makes it worse. I used to repeat in my head, *She's not giving me a hard time; she's having a hard time.* That helped me shift my mindset to see that something was blocking her, and my job was to help, not judge. Staying calm means taking judgment and blame out of it, but it's human nature to do both.

Q: When Willow is panicking, how do you communicate with her?

A: Penny: When she was younger, leaving her alone made her feel rejected, so I'd stay with her. But by middle and high school, she preferred me to give her space. I'm a fixer, so if I saw she was emotional, I'd say, "Let's talk about this and fix it." But that only added pressure. I've learned that you have to let them come to you when they're ready. I call it co-escalation versus co-regulation. You can either escalate things by reacting emotionally, or you can offer calm and show them how to manage whatever they're dealing with.

Q: So you've learned what not to do through experience.

A: Penny: Yes, and when parents ask me what I used to do, I admit I sometimes yelled back. But I know better now. Yelling doesn't help; it just escalates the situation.

Q: Willow, what advice do you have for parents who want to help their child during a panic?

A: Willow: Stay calm and don't start shouting. Let it all out calmly.

A: Penny: And it doesn't need to be resolved right away.

A: Willow: Yeah, that's true.

A: Penny: Willow taught me that sometimes you don't have to tackle everything immediately. Time makes things more doable. I'd ask how her day was, and she'd say, "I don't want to talk about it." So I'd try again later. She even quit family dinner for a while because she felt interrogated.

Q: I understand that. My son is the same way.

A: Willow: I don't like answering questions if I'm not in the mood. If you ask me something and I don't want to answer, I'll just say, "I don't want to talk about it." Asking more questions only makes it worse. I don't want to be questioned.

Q: What advice do you have for a family with a child who has ADHD or autism? How do they know if the school is not the right place?

A: Penny: You'll know the school is bad if it's not just one or two teachers causing anxiety, but the entire faculty is perpetuating it. If you're working your way up the chain of command—from the teacher to the vice principal and then to the principal—and no one understands the problem, that's a red flag. In that case, get out of that school immediately.

Q: Are there in-home strategies parents can use?

A: Penny: Start with the relationship. If it's all pressure and stress, the relationship with your child can break down. They stop trusting you, and you stop trusting them. You need to reestablish that trust. Let your child know 100 percent that you get it, that you value them, and that you're there to help. That shift in the dynamic can make a huge difference. They may open up more about what's bothering them and be more willing to try therapy or give school another shot. When nothing's working, lower the demand drastically—that's a sign that they can't handle the current pressure or expectations.

Give them something they can succeed at, even if it's as simple as getting out of bed or leaving the house. Celebrate the small wins. Make sure they feel successful at something, even if school isn't working out right now.

CHAPTER 9

Tools for Parents

Understanding Parental Accommodations and SPACE Therapy

Throughout the book, we've talked about accommodations with schools, IEPs, and 504 plans. Those accommodations make it possible for your child to access their education—like going to a school staff member's office when feeling overwhelmed or getting extra time on assignments and tests. Those are school-related accommodations you can request from your school's intervention team, 504 committee, or IEP team if they help your child succeed.

Parental Accommodations

The accommodations addressed here focus on the parent-child dynamic. They are the things parents may do in an attempt to protect, shield, and help their children avoid anxiety or distress. Dina Nunziato, PhD, chief clinical director of the Anxiety Institute, clarifies and explains:

Parental accommodation occurs when parents change their behavior to relieve their child's distress or anxiety. First, it's completely natural. Parents are hard-wired to respond to their child's distress. The higher the child's distress, the more inclined parents are to accommodate. The not-so-good news is that parental accommodation can backfire and create a negative cycle. This occurs when parents accommodate their child's anxiety and inadvertently send messages to their child that 1) their child's anxiety is something to be feared, and 2) that they don't trust the child to manage their anxiety. By removing the source of the anxiety, and by depriving the child of the opportunity to manage their own feelings, the child's anxiety is reinforced. This pattern of accommodation sends the message that it's okay or necessary to respond to anxiety in this way. It gives anxiety power that it doesn't deserve and wouldn't otherwise have. It unintentionally sends the signal that parents don't believe in their child's ability to cope, that the child needs to be protected, and that the child may be vulnerable or weak. Although no one is doing this intentionally, accommodation of this type maintains and escalates anxiety symptoms.

Three Common Accommodation Traps

- An overabundance of blanket reassurance through statements like "Everything will be okay," or "Don't worry, it will all work out." Although it's perfectly okay to convey reassurance periodically, repeated blanket reassurance does not validate the realities of everyday life.

- Allowing the child to create situations in which the entire family is avoiding a problem so the child's anxiety is not triggered.
- Excessive assistance with decisions and simple tasks that the child can develop the ability to do for themself.

Considering the child's developmental stage is critical when addressing accommodations. This looks very different for parents of young children than for older adolescents or young adults. Determining the level of support that your child needs is often the first step in reducing accommodations. For example, early adolescents may need direct assistance in managing difficult emotions, whereas teens may respond to statements of confidence in their ability to utilize emotion-regulation skills.

Parenting Styles

The following are some differing parenting styles that are broadly overstated, but you might recognize some that mirror your own way of reacting to your child.

The Pusher

"The Pusher" is a parent who believes all issues are behavioral and that managing anxiety is completely about facing your fears—"If they're afraid of swimming, throw them in the water," that sort of thing. This style often fails because it's emotionally invalidating, and unless it is done skillfully and gradually, it will lead to failure.

The Pusher may say things like "I'm going to call the attendance officer," or "You used to be able to go to school. You can go now." The positive aspect of this approach is that you are encouraging your child to face their fear; however, it's very invalidating and may backfire against you and what you want for your child.

The Softy

"The Softy" is in many ways the opposite of the Pusher and may say things like "What's the matter, honey? If you feel sick, it's okay. Why don't you stay home today?" The positive aspect of this type of response is that it taps into the parent's basic instinct to protect their child. The child does feel understood and validated. However, this approach does not allow the child to develop resilience skills, since the parent is inadvertently sending a message that the child is not capable of managing the situation and needs to be overly protected. In this way, the Softy inadvertently perpetuates a pattern of avoidance.

The Anticipator

"The Anticipator" looks ahead and tries to prevent anxiety-provoking situations. These parents are attempting to be empathic by anticipating the child's feelings and being aware of their limitations. But it doesn't work. The Anticipator's approach models avoidance as the primary strategy for managing anxiety. For example, if there's a school band competition, you'll have your child stay home and say things like "I don't think that's such a good idea. I'm going to tell them you can't go."

The Ideal

"The Ideal" parenting model is one we all aspire to, of course, but no one is perfect. The Ideal focuses on pushing compassionately and supporting competency, including communicating that physical symptoms can be tolerated. This means your child can have a (mild) stomachache and still move forward. Or your child can have a bit of a headache, but they can still move forward and be realistic about their limitations without shutting down completely.

You might say something like "I know you're not feeling well. This usually happens when you have a big test. I know it's hard, but I know you can do this. Think of how proud you will be of yourself when it's all over."

More Dos and Don'ts of Accommodation

- **Don't** remove stressors that trigger anxiety or avoid things because they make your child anxious.
- **Do** respect feelings without causing feelings to overly impact behavior.
- **Don't** ask leading questions.
- **Do** express positive, realistic expectations.
- **Don't** reinforce your child's fears.

Supportive Parenting for Anxious Childhood Emotions (SPACE)

Most experienced therapists who help children with anxiety and school avoidance will discuss reducing parental accommodations as part of their child's treatment. They discuss the unintentional negative role of parental accommodation as it affects school-avoidance outcomes. To paraphrase Dr. Dina Nunziato, these are natural and normal reactions since every parent wants to prevent their child from feeling uncomfortable and anxious. It is in our nature to protect our children. So, going against this instinct is challenging. This is where SPACE treatment comes into play.

Dr. Eli Lebowitz, a psychologist at the Yale Child Study Center, developed SPACE (Supportive Parenting for Anxious Childhood Emotions), which has been proven effective in clinical trials and in real life based on feedback from clinicians and families. The program offers strategies to help parents support anxious children without the need for the child to attend therapy. The focus is on reducing parental accommodations that maintain the child's anxiety.

As a parent-based therapy, SPACE can improve communication between you and your child while helping them return to learning. Dr. Rebecca Etkin, a clinical psychologist at the Yale Child Study Center and a leading trainer of SPACE, shared her insights with me. She has worked with over a hundred families using SPACE and explains how it can be beneficial for families dealing with school avoidance.

What Is SPACE?

SPACE is a fully parent-based treatment for childhood anxiety disorders. And when I say anxiety disorders, that includes things like generalized anxiety disorder, separation anxiety disorder, social anxiety disorder, and obsessive-compulsive disorder. Parts of SPACE can be useful for anxiety-related problems like school avoidance.

Fully parent-based means only parents attend the treatment sessions and implement the treatment tools. That makes SPACE unique compared to any other evidence-based anxiety treatment approach. Pretty much every other approach that has a solid evidence base behind it does entail that the child at least attends some of the sessions or changes some of their behaviors, thoughts, and feelings, so this is a unique way of going about treatment.

Q: Is there a structure to the treatment?

A: Dr. Etkin: SPACE is what we call a manualized treatment, meaning that it has specified components that should be followed to say, "Okay, we've implemented this treatment with fidelity." In other words, if we implement it in this way, we have evidence that it can be effective. SPACE is broken down into different parts that cover different content, tools, and strategies. It doesn't have to be so highly structured that you are saying for session one, "You must do this." But it will be most effective if all of the parts are implemented in order.

Actually, what I love about SPACE is that it is very flexible. Even though it's manualized and structured in terms of the parts you should cover, it can be tailored for each family and their unique circumstances and needs. The therapist can also be flexible in terms of their style and how they implement SPACE.

The Two Main Pillars of SPACE

1. Increasing supportive parental responses to child anxiety.
2. Decreasing accommodations for child anxiety.

Q: Can you explain the components of SPACE treatment?

A: Dr. Etkin: We start with what we call **setting the stage for treatment**. It's essential that we spend some time talking to parents about why we're doing parent-based treatment. Because I think a lot of parents could understandably have misconceptions, like, okay, if you want to meet with me, it must mean that I'm to blame or I'm the cause of my child's anxiety. And that's exacerbated by so much societal and public discourse about parent blaming and shaming.

And so, we want to dispel any myth we're meeting with parents because we think parents are the problem. We're meeting with parents because we know that when there is an anxious child who has the tendency to be anxious, primarily for biological reasons, they're going to naturally draw parents into their anxiety. Because the most natural thing in the world is for an anxious child to say, "Mom and Dad, help me. Help me not feel so anxious, help me avoid, help me escape." And then, as a parent, what do you do?

We believe, and this is supported by research, too, that parents are not the problem but are an important part of the solution. They're always going to be inherently drawn into their child's anxiety. And so, to say that parents are irrelevant to child anxiety treatment is silly.

As an adult, I'm afraid to go to work and anxious about work. I can just avoid it. I could stay home. But if you're a child scared to go to school, you need parents to be involved with that avoidance process. Or parents are going to be at least involved in the back-and-forth about "No, you need to go to school," maybe trying to encourage you to go to school and ultimately letting you stay home or basically dragging you in. Parents are always involved, so we want to spell that out and say because there is that back-and-forth between them and dealing with the child's anxiety, if the parent is the one to make changes in how they respond, that will inherently change the child. We can do this whole treatment by involving parents because parents and children are a system, and if the parents are the ones to make some changes on their end, it will impact their child. So we don't have to ask the child to come to sessions. We don't have to ask the child to change their behavior. Parents will do everything, which is great because adults can be in control of their own behavior. And we're still going to help the child. Many parents feel liberated when they hear that because I'll ask them, "What have you tried to help your child?" And they'll say, "I've told them to take a deep breath, but then they don't want to take a deep breath." Or they say, "Taking a deep breath doesn't work." That's an attempt to try to sort of control or direct what the child is doing, and some children will go along with it, and that's great and helpful, but a lot of children won't or can't, and so then it leaves parents, once again, in the tricky position of "Okay, how do I help?" SPACE is empowering because it gives parents the tools: "Here's what I can do, and by doing these things, I'm still going to help my child."

Using Supportive Responses to Anxiety

That's part one of laying the groundwork and starts the discussion about these supportive responses to anxiety, so we coach parents, when in the face of your child's anxiety, to really try to express some understanding or validation or acceptance of the anxiety. For example, say, "Your anxiety is a real thing. We get it. It's hard, it's painful." This expression of validation is integrated with an expression of confidence that the child can handle their anxiety. It's not always very intuitive for people to say. Especially when they don't necessarily have a lot of confidence that their child can cope very well with anxiety to still be able to say, "I see you're anxious right now. I get it, and that's hard, *but I believe that you have the power to handle that type of feeling, and you'll get through it.*"

Over time, we find that using these sorts of statements in the face of a child's anxiety begins to shift the child's own relationship with their anxiety because they feel like "Okay, I have these feelings, they're normal, my parent gets them, they're okay, but I can get through these feelings. These feelings don't have to be threatening. They don't have to overcome me." It really starts to open a child's world because then they're not always running away from their feelings.

Sometimes, I'll be working with a family, and we don't even get to the accommodation part of treatment because just by parents starting to use these statements, the child is so much more willing to face their fears and do hard things. The child begins to think, *Anxious feelings are something that I can live with and handle. I can feel anxious and go to school at the same time.*

That's of course not always the case; sometimes, a parent will say one of these statements, and the child responds, "No, I can't handle those feelings," or "You don't know what you're talking about." It's fine. The supportive statement is the first step in the parents changing their own behavior by simply stating their belief: I believe you are anxious, and I believe you can handle anxiety. They don't have to try to convince their child. They don't have to get into an argument. If their child says, "No, that's not true," the parent can say, "Okay, well, that's what I believe about you."

We see time and time again how powerful and helpful these simple statements are. Some parents feel it sounds cheesy or unnatural, and I get it. That's only sometimes how we talk to children. We might more naturally say the first part—I understand you're anxious—but then we go into problem-solving mode, such as "You're anxious. Why don't you take deep breaths or cuddle your stuffed animal?" There's nothing wrong with that, but it's saying, "Okay, I understand you're anxious, so do this thing to try not to be anxious," versus "I believe you can handle being anxious. I think it's okay to be anxious."

Q: Are there times when you should not be using these statements, for example, in the heat of the moment?

A: Dr. Etkin: It's NEVER NOT ACCEPTABLE to use these statements. It can be even more useful in the heat of an anxious moment when it's often most difficult for parents to think of something consistent and helpful to say. If parents have concerns, I'll say, "Tell me what your child is going to say when you say this," "What's going to be hard for you about saying this?," "What's going to get in the way?" We work through it for each family, so we tailor it, come up with language that feels a little more natural to the parent, and practice. We have strategies for how parents implement these statements because we don't want them arguing with their children or trying to convince them. They have to say it, and that's it. And maybe then give their children some space. For example, "I'll give you a minute and check back with you." We coach parents around all potential challenges that could arise. This can make it easier and more practical for parents to use supportive statements even in the heat of difficult moments.

Q: What makes confidence so powerful when helping children with anxiety and school avoidance?

A: **Dr. Etkin:** The confidence component helps children feel they don't have to push their anxious feelings away. Because as a child, if I feel my number one goal is not to feel anxious, then I'm going to do whatever I can to avoid anything that scares me. But if I recognize I have this anxiety, while it doesn't feel great, I can handle it. I can still go to school and have the anxiety at the exact same time, and I'll be okay. It's big. We don't ask children not to feel anxious. We don't ask them to try to push away their anxiety. We're saying, let your anxiety be there, and we know that you'll be okay. Of course, not every tool works for every family, but these supportive statements, on average, make a big difference and a big part of treatment.

Charting Accommodations

The next part of SPACE is to teach parents what accommodation is, why parents do it, how normal and natural it is, but how sometimes it may not be the most helpful thing. Then, we want to work with parents to identify how they feel they are accommodating.

For example, in terms of morning time, we want to know precisely what the mornings look like. How early does your morning start? What do you do? What does your child do?

We refer to this step as **charting accommodations**. We want to go through a typical day, and we want parents to start to identify all the different things they're doing in response to their child's anxiety in order to alleviate it or prevent it.

Then from that process, the next step is identifying a target that we want to work on because we do not want parents to think they must change everything on that chart at a time. It wouldn't be helpful, it wouldn't be therapeutic, and it wouldn't be possible. So, we zoom in on an accommodation the parents feel would make such a big difference in their and their child's life.

We pick a target and start there. For example, a parent spends thirty minutes sitting with their child in bed every morning, trying to talk them out of feeling anxious. And that's what we want to change.

The next step after choosing a target is making a detailed, very specific plan to change what's happening to reduce the accommodation. And again, this is where it's highly tailored to the family and their circumstance. We want parents to tell us everything that could go wrong, everything that could make it hard, and we want parents to be thinking ten steps ahead so that they don't start out with this plan that sounds nice in theory, and then they're like, no, this isn't going to work.

Once we formulate a plan to reduce accommodation, parents implement it and report back. They may tweak it if they need to. They talk about what made it difficult or easy, and then the rest of the treatment repeats this process: going back to the accommodation list, picking another target, updating the list if necessary, picking another target, and making another plan.

Even if you come in and your child is very anxious and you're accommodating in a million ways, you only typically need to target two or maybe three accommodations because there's a process of generalization that occurs. You're starting to show the child you know that even though they're anxious, you believe they can handle it so much that you are not going to always accommodate the anxiety. And so, the child is starting to get better. They're beginning to learn that they can face their fears. They can do hard things. They can cope. And so, you don't have to target everything on your list; you do two or three things, and the child gets better.

Short-Term Therapy

That's why this can be a short-term treatment. I do therapy a lot in the context of Dr. Eli Lebowitz's clinical trials, and in a clinical trial, a family gets twelve sessions, and it's very regimented. I find that twelve sessions are often enough because we'll do the work on support, and we'll talk a lot about anxiety. We'll make two or three plans to reduce accommodation, and the child will be better or well on their way. And even if there are still some things to target, the parents know the process now. They've learned the tools to identify how they're accommodating: This is how I plan to change my behavior, so I'm not accommodating. Here's how I can support my child so they can continue this process on their own or in the future if they need to.

Q: Do you have some examples of accommodations you work with for school avoidance families?

A: Dr. Etkin: One of the things that I see the most in the families I work with is parents accommodating by picking their child up from school early. These kids can get to school, but maybe they text their parents during the day. I don't feel well. I'm anxious. I'm having a panic attack. Or maybe parents get a call from the school nurse who maybe doesn't understand anxiety as well, or something like that, and the parent picks the child up. That's accommodation because parents are leaving their work and changing their behavior to come pick their child up. What that does is maybe it sends an inadvertent message, telling the child, "You're right. I don't think you can handle your anxiety. I need to come get you." Another common accommodation is when parents respond to messages while the child is at school. The child is texting. So now the parent is taking time out of their day to write back. We consider that an accommodation. They're changing their own behavior to try to alleviate their child's anxiety. I worked with one family whose whole life became an accommodation because the mom took the child out of school. He was having a tough time going to school due to anxiety, so she switched him out of school to homeschooling. Sometimes, that is the right choice for a family, and sometimes, maybe the parent feels like their hand is forced. In another family I worked with, the parents felt like they had to use a lot of bribery and promises. For example, I'll take you to Starbucks on your way to school. Or, if you go to school today, you don't have to go tomorrow. Again, these are attempts by the parents to reduce the anxiety a little and just get the child to do what they need them to do.

Parents often describe accommodations as feeling between a rock and a hard place. By emailing the school administration or teacher on behalf of the child, going and picking up work from the school for the child, or calling classmates' parents to get notes for the child, you are making a lot of calls and doing a lot of behind-the-scenes work on behalf of the child that could be considered an accommodation. These actions alleviate the child's anxiety, and the child doesn't have to do the things that scare them.

Q: How do we reduce accommodation, such as when parents email the teacher or the school? This is one I personally couldn't do with my child.

A: Dr. Etkin: This is the meat of SPACE: when we're sitting down to plan, and we say the accommodation is that currently the parent is, at least three times a week, emailing the teacher. So, what's a plan to change that? It would really depend on the specific circumstances of the family and the school. But we would always want to help the parents figure out what they are going to do instead, how much or often, and how they are going to manage any difficult reactions from their child. One thing we would also do is get the teachers and the school involved as what we would refer to in SPACE as supporters. In SPACE, we make use of other people outside of the immediate family. This could be neighbors, parents of the child's friends, extended family members, teachers, coaches, or anyone who cares about the child and might be willing to help a little bit. We might draw them in to help implement plans or to help address barriers that might arise with plans.

Q: Is it advisable to tell your child that you are working on reducing accommodations?

A: Dr. Etkin: Yes. That is the next step. We always want to be extremely transparent in this treatment. There's no point in surprising the child with a change in parents' behavior. In the flow of SPACE, you choose a target, plan to reduce the target's accommodation, and then inform the child. We inform the child in a really special way, which is with a written letter.

Many parents and therapists feel this is weird, overly formal, and unusual, but that's where the power lies. It signifies, okay, this isn't just another lecture. This isn't just us saying again that you must go to school. We've really been careful about making a plan. For two-parent families who have been a little polarized in their approach to the child, this is an excellent moment for them to unify and say that they both agree this is the way for them to move forward and help their child. And it's a lovely supportive letter, but it lets the child know what they can expect.

For example, in the letter, we call this announcing the plan to the child or informing the child of the plan. It might sound like "Dear Sally, we know that when you think you're behind on your schoolwork, you get nervous and want Mom to email the teacher for you. We understand that lots of kids feel that way, but we realize that if we keep emailing the teacher for you, we're not actually helping you feel less anxious. We're making it worse because we're not showing how much we believe in you. From now on, we won't be emailing your teacher anymore. We will always ensure you stay caught up in school." (Or you can put other assurances in.) The teacher would be a part of this plan. The parents may have a behind-the-scenes plan for the teacher to check in with the child the next day, email them, and say, "Hey, Sally, I see you haven't turned in your homework. Can I help?" And it won't impact their grades initially because we're giving this plan a chance.

If this child is so avoidant of their teacher and schoolwork, it might be an excellent place to show the child you know your teacher cares. Your teacher isn't going to be mad. Your teacher is invested in you and keeps you from falling behind. But maybe this isn't going to happen through the whole school year; this is just a starting place. This will allow parents to stick with their plan of not having to email the teacher. It relieves that pressure on them because the teacher will take over. If Sally says, "Email my teacher," Mom says, "Remember, I know you're anxious. I believe you can handle it. Remember, I'm not going to be emailing your teacher. If you want to, you can feel free to do so. I believe you can do it." But she's not forcing Sally to email the teacher. And then, if Sally does amazing, we can praise that. And if Sally doesn't, okay, that was Sally's choice, and we know the contingency plan is that the teacher will check in the next day if the teacher is willing to do that. That plan might not work for every family, but it allows parents to start to take that step back and send the message that *I'm not going to keep feeding your anxiety by doing this for you, but we're also not going to let you fall off the grid in terms of school.* Something along those lines is an example of a plan I've made with families.

Q: Are there some roadblocks and speed bumps that trip up families?

A: Dr. Etkin: One of the most challenging roadblocks is when kids get aggressive when parents stop accommodating. Many anxious kids go into fight-or-flight mode, and fighting is part of that, and yes, that can challenge families. I worked with a child who had obsessive-compulsive disorder, and he was terrified of this one song. And every time he heard the song, he freaked out, so the whole family couldn't play the radio; they couldn't turn it on. His teacher was having fun using music in class, and he wouldn't go to school because of this. We planned to work on this. Part of it was the parents saying, "We're no longer going to accommodate by keeping the house silent; if someone feels like listening to music, they're allowed to listen." And this child would get aggressive; he would throw things and sometimes run out of the house. It was a problematic roadblock for this family. They were worried about him being aggressive at school. So again, every circumstance is unique, but we would have to coach parents through that: If your child becomes aggressive, what will you do? How do we de-escalate the situation as quickly and safely as possible? That usually entails removing everyone else from the situation instead of trying to calm down an aggressive child. We would work through that with each family.

Q: I would have been the parent who called the school and said they could not play that song in my child's class. What would you say to parents who would want to call the teacher and request that the music is not played?

A: Dr. Etkin: That's understandable and natural because you don't want your child to face that or be distressed. This is why accommodation is so natural. Ultimately, we would want to weigh whether it is more helpful than not helpful. What message is it sending your child about their capacity to handle anxiety and how threatening anxiety is if you enact that accommodation?

Q: You don't advise schools to take away accommodations all at once, cold turkey, and be like, *good luck, kid*, do you?

A: Dr. Etkin: Right, because how you get rid of an accommodation is important, and that's why I think so many parents would benefit from this treatment. If you tell a parent that we know accommodating isn't so helpful, just don't do it, a parent will feel that their child is going to freak out, and they're not going to get anything done. We need to go through it carefully—that's the whole point of SPACE. We need to go through how we reduce the accommodation, how we communicate it to the child, and how we help the parent feel empowered to follow through.

Q: Does a parent need a therapist to do SPACE?

A: Dr. Etkin: The book *Breaking Free of Child Anxiety and OCD* by Dr.

Eli Lebowitz was written for parents to use as a self-help book, so parents don't necessarily need a therapist. However, many parents prefer a therapist to guide them through these challenging steps. As a parent, you might know that you are the kind of person who would benefit from having someone guide you through this or just someone to check in with every week to keep you on track.

Q: I have seen some SPACE therapists advertising to treat a group of families together. What do you think about those?

A: **Dr. Etkin:** They're great. I have run a group, and there are a lot of benefits to groups. One benefit is having that sense of connection with other parents who are going through the same thing. It can feel very isolating to have a child who's struggling with anxiety or school avoidance, and you also often feel blamed. Connecting with other parents can make you feel supported. And sometimes, in groups, parents end up being supporters of each other on their plans.

I have seen two types of SPACE groups. One type of SPACE group works through all the steps of treatment in detail with the families, and so the group has to be on the smaller side and otherwise equipped to do it so that each family gets that personalized attention. Another type of group we've seen is more what we call an informational or psychoeducational SPACE group. In this kind of group, the main tools and principles are presented to the families, but then it's up to them to implement them. It does not necessarily entail doing every step with every family in the group. If families know what they're getting and what they're signed up for, both types of groups could be helpful.

Q: Can you remind me of the website to find SPACE-trained providers?

A: **Dr. Etkin:** spacetreatment [dot] net.

Q: Are many therapists getting trained in SPACE?

A: **Dr. Etkin:** Yes, there are a lot, spread out around the country, and all over the world. We estimate that there are about four thousand SPACE-trained clinicians at this time!

Q: What about training for schools?

A: **Dr. Etkin:** Schools are interested, and we are actively working on developing a SPACE model and associated training for schools. Some parts of the treatment are more easily adapted to the school context than others. For example, anyone who works in a school could use a supportive statement. The issue of reducing accommodation is a little more nuanced. Some school psychologists have more time, resources, and availability to work with parents to reduce accommodation. Some schools, as you know, are so strapped and don't have as much time and resources to dedicate to helping parents with this process, so there's a lot of variability. Accommodations also typically mean something slightly different in the school context—such as supports that are granted through 504 and IEP plans. So, it may take more thought and coordination to disentangle which accommodations that are being granted are helpful or less helpful for reducing the child's anxiety so that they can function better at school.

Q: A lot of therapists experienced in treating children with school avoidance will explain the negative effects of parental accommodations. How is SPACE different?

A: Dr. Etkin: Other treatment approaches discuss accommodations and, more broadly, how parents might inadvertently contribute to their child's avoidance of scary things.

Accommodation really has an effect: It enables the child to keep avoiding and fuels anxiety. But, reducing accommodation is not always intuitive or easy. What is different about SPACE is how it clarifies how to identify accommodations, how to reduce them, how to help families think through all the roadblocks and challenges, and how to engage other supports to help you in the process.

CHAPTER 10

The Dreaded T-Word

Truancy

For parents of children with school avoidance, the struggle with attendance is not just a legal requirement—it is an emotional battle. We would do almost anything to get our child to go to school; we dream about it and long for it. It's a daily fight against fear and worry, as we never know what to expect when we walk into our child's bedroom to ensure that they're up for school.

Parents understand that school avoidance can severely limit their child's future opportunities. The negative impact on their learning, education, and post-high-school options is a constant worry. We know that education is key, and the fear of our children's futures being compromised due to school avoidance is a heavy burden.

However, attendance is the law for school administrators, legislators, prosecutors, and the juvenile justice system, as outlined by compulsory education and truancy laws. To these stakeholders, school attendance is nonnegotiable, where the realities of school avoidance have not been recognized. Post–COVID-19, growing rates of chronic absenteeism have drawn more attention from stakeholders, but there remains a huge disconnect. The gap between compulsory education laws and school avoidance persists because few stakeholders understand what school avoidance is and why these children are often still treated as truants.

Compulsory Education

The first compulsory education law in the United States was passed in 1642 in the Massachusetts Bay Colony. It stemmed from the Puritans' belief that education was a moral and social obligation. The law recognized free public education as a societal duty.

By 1918, all states had enacted school attendance legislation. As populations increased and the demand for skilled labor grew, bureaucratic systems for enforcement were established.

These laws exist to protect children and ensure that there is access to public education. They're particularly beneficial for children from families that might otherwise pull them out of school for caregiving, work, or other reasons. Each state has compulsory attendance laws, which limit the number of absences a child can have. States vary in their definitions of truancy, but the unease school-avoidance families feel about compulsory education laws stems from the fact that they translate into truancy threats.

Truancy and the Law

The label "truant" presents another significant challenge for families dealing with school avoidance. Julian G. Elliott of Durham University and

Maurice Place of Northumbria University note, "A complicating feature of the school refusal/truancy distinction is that some forms of nonattendance are viewed more sympathetically than others, likely affecting adult responses. Due to the legal nature of the term and its association with conduct disorder, those deemed truant may be seen as culpable. The impact of labeling can result in differential access to professional services and forms of intervention, with truancy more likely to lead to legal proceedings, which often reflect a punitive rather than therapeutic focus."

The truth is truancy laws can wreak havoc on families of school-avoidant children. These laws don't distinguish between truancy and school avoidance, and unfortunately, many schools don't, either. This causes unnecessary stress and fear for families. Since school avoidance isn't recognized as an excused absence, truancy laws often expose and penalize families, triggering the dreaded attendance letter. For parents of school-avoidant children, these letters feel like threats of truancy court.

Attendance Letters and Truancy Threats

If your child has school avoidance, you've likely received these letters. Although well-intentioned, they often feel accusatory and threatening to parents. Typically, they contain:

- A record of your child's absences.
- A reiteration of your state's truancy laws, citing specific statutes.
- A reminder of the importance of school attendance for your child's future.
- The potential consequences.

Schools may list the exact dates your child was absent, which can feel overwhelming for parents who have long struggled with school avoidance. But the scariest part is the consequences, which often seem unfair.

Common penalties in truancy letters include:

- Fines, sometimes as high as $500.
- Loss of driving privileges for the child.
- Community service for the parent or the child.
- Jail time for parents, up to thirty days.
- Referral to truancy court.
- Requiring the parent to accompany the child to school.
- Requiring the child and parent/guardian to sign a contract agreeing to regular attendance.

While these letters are intended to address chronic absenteeism, they often feel like a punch in the stomach to families dealing with school avoidance. They evoke emotions of fear, frustration, and even anger—feelings that are completely valid and understandable.

Truancy letters are typically automated and are sent out when a student accumulates a specific number of unexcused absences within a certain period. The threshold for sending these letters varies by state, county, or school district. It may be triggered after three, five, or ten absences.

Generally, most schools define a child as chronically absent if they miss 10 percent or more of school days. Some schools use a benchmark of consecutive days absent, while others consider the total number of days missed, regardless of whether the absences are consecutive.

Because these letters are often sent automatically, the school administration may not review them before they're sent to parents. Many schools don't realize how cold and threatening these letters can feel to families dealing with school avoidance.

If you're working with your school to address your child's school avoidance, you may want to ask them to stop sending these attendance letters. Depending on the school, they might agree easily, or they may respond that the letters are automatically generated and cannot be stopped. Usually, the letters are controlled by a software system that can be adjusted if necessary. In some cases, attendance clerks send them manually, and they, too, can be instructed to stop. It's up to you whether you want to request that your school stop sending you these absentee notifications.

Because chronic absenteeism is such a problem and schools are starting to understand that mental health and school avoidance are real impediments to attendance, schools are re-evaluating the language in these letters to show families they genuinely care and want to help. School superintendents, principals, assistant principals, directors of special education, or special services set the tone for how their staff responds to families of school-avoidant children regarding referrals to truancy court and everything involved in assisting those families appropriately and effectively.

Schools do have the discretion and ability to prevent school-avoidant students and their families from suffering truancy consequences. "School districts have the option to file a truancy citation with the courts. However, researchers, public officials, and advocates agree taking families to court is not mandatory, and it's often the wrong way to go. It is an option to refer a family for truancy court. It is not a requirement," said Hetal Dhagat, a Pittsburgh-based lawyer with the Education Law Center. All schools vary in their views and, therefore, their use of referring families to truancy court for absenteeism. We have heard of school districts referring as many as a hundred students to truancy court a year and others that have referred one or none. If a school or district refers many students to truancy court each year, it is pretty telling that they do not understand school avoidance or the reasons children are truant and don't have appropriate or effective interventions in place to help these students and their families.

Attendance Policy

Families of children with school avoidance will often ask their school to modify the attendance policy while working to get their child back to regularly attending school. You may hear an emphatic "No, that's our attendance policy, and we can't change it." However, school leadership can modify attendance if warranted, as in school-avoidance cases. If they are reluctant to do this, they may say, "It's the law, and we must follow compulsory education laws, and that is our attendance policy. We don't change that for anyone." But just like it is up to their discretion to refer students and families to truancy court, it is up to them to modify your child's attendance.

If your school refuses to modify attendance as you work to get your child back to school, they don't get it. But you still may be able to find one champion in your school to help remove this barrier and help your child get back to school. Also, it is possible they will not say they are officially modifying the attendance policy for you, but your social worker or case manager may alter attendance as you are working to reintegrate your child back into school.

Excused and Unexcused Absences

Excused and unexcused absences are another part of attendance policies that school-avoidance families face: worrying that their child will accrue unexcused absences, leading to truancy threats, failing classes, and other consequences.

When an absence is labeled unexcused, it can affect a child's opportunities to make up missed work and can lead to failing grades in classes. When children are absent, schools use attendance codes to determine whether the absence is excused or unexcused. Of course, there is currently no code for school avoidance. Some schools, however, are starting to include codes for behavioral health that may include attendance challenges.

When a Doctor's Note Is Required

Fortunately, some states have updated their attendance laws to include mental health as an excused absence, just like physical illness. For example, California's Education Code allows for excused absences due to mental or behavioral health issues.

However, many schools still require a doctor's note to excuse an absence. This requirement can be inequitable and invalidating, especially for families without health insurance or those whose children suffer from mental health conditions. It makes little sense for a child with anxiety or depression to need a note from a pediatrician to excuse their absence.

Some states, like Massachusetts, Texas, and Illinois, have reduced the need for a doctor's note, allowing parents to excuse absences for up to five days without one. After five days, however, schools in these states may require a doctor's note. If this becomes an issue, you might consider speaking with your school's administration about waiving the requirement for your child's mental health needs.

Protecting Yourself

In addition to everything we covered in chapters 3 and 4 about working with your school and your child's right to an education regardless of disability, you can protect yourself from truancy court by documenting your efforts and the work you've done to help your child. It's essential to keep copies of all your emails to your school about your child's school avoidance and any requests for assistance. Also, maintain a record of therapists, programs, professionals, and doctors consulted, along with the dates or time frames of those interactions. Don't forget to document conversations as well. Taking contemporaneous notes—written records made as soon as possible after an event or discussion—can be extremely valuable. These notes should include details such as the date and time of the event, who was present, and what was said or observed.

Yes, this can feel like an extra burden when you're already overwhelmed trying to support your child. If keeping such detailed records feels like too much, don't be hard on yourself——give yourself grace. This advice comes from attorneys, advocates, and other families who have navigated school avoidance and truancy challenges, and it's meant to empower you, not overwhelm you.

Journalist and education reporter Tylisa C. Johnson shared a helpful suggestion in an article on common misconceptions about truancy:

> Parents, guardians, or students have multiple chances to show evidence or explain why a student is struggling with attendance or has valid reasons for missing school, both before and in court. When initially cited as truant, parents and students can show evidence that absences were justified, such as a religious holiday or tutoring, or push for the school to develop a school attendance improvement plan and advocate for support and services to address attendance barriers. If parents end up before a judge, they can still bring proof such as doctor's notes, correspondence with school staff, or other items that show they took "every reasonable step" to ensure the student's attendance. Students and families can also appeal fines and other court orders.

A parent in our School Avoidance Alliance community shares that this strategy worked for her:

> List all of the medication you tried, when you went up in doses, when you tried another one. List every time you asked the school for help and what the outcome of that is. Bring doctor's notes with diagnoses, bring information about school avoidance, bring it all. While my son was in front of the judge with his court lawyer, I raised my hand a lot and the judge let me talk. I brought multiple copies of my timeline to share with the judge, our lawyer and the truant officer. Our school joined by video conference and when they said something false, I raised my hand and politely corrected their statement to the judge. We got a 90-day period of review at which point the claim was dismissed. The judge specifically said to the truant officer that he filed a child requiring assistance and clearly, I was assisting my son. He said he didn't see any additional assistance that the court could offer at this time.

The Perception of Truancy

Another complexity of school avoidance and a thorn in our side is the whole concept of truancy. Because most schools are not educated on what school avoidance means and how it differs from truancy, they refer to our children's absenteeism as truancy.

Truancy has the connotation of bad behavior and delinquent children. When absenteeism is painted with the same brush, generalizing all absent children as truant invokes negative feelings in children and parents who don't care about education. Of course, the worst part is that our children are being treated punitively. In addition to truancy court, some schools go as far as unenrolling students absent for ten days or more, removing the student's access to their online classwork, or refusing to grade or acknowledge schoolwork submitted while absent.

Schools Need to Learn How to Distinguish School Avoidance from Truancy

Unfortunately, schools may incorrectly refer to a child's school avoidance as truancy. Dina Nunziato, PhD, chief clinical director of the Anxiety Institute, explains that schools must understand that children with school avoidance seek comfort. And home is typically that place of comfort and security. They may want to remain close to parental figures, especially if they offer safety and security. They may want to stay in their room. Again, they're trying to establish a sense of safety and security. They can become upset at the prospect of having to attend school.

The emotional upset may take the form of actual emotional expression and often of unexplained physical symptoms, headaches, stomachaches, and exhaustion. There are no major antisocial tendencies. The only thing we might see in terms of something we might call antisocial is aggression, which may come out if the child is being forced to go to school. There is no attempt to conceal that child's not going to school. The child makes it known that they're fearful of going to school and don't want to. With truancy, there's more hiding and more trying to get away with something. It's not anxiety-based. It's not a function of emotional distress. It tends to be motivated more by pleasure and is usually concealed from parents.

Punitive Responses

Unfortunately, schools commonly respond to school avoidance with penalization and punishment. These penalties can range from exclusion from extracurricular activities and loss of course credit, to failing grades, mandatory Saturday school, and even being sent to truancy court. Research and real life show that punitive responses don't work and, in fact, even make matters worse.

> "The current, court-centered approach to addressing truancy is not working—students are criminalized at an alarmingly high rate, often for behavior that is completely out of their control. Other indicators like attendance rates have not significantly improved despite the high numbers of court filings."
>
> —DEBORAH FOWLER, EXECUTIVE DIRECTOR OF TEXAS APPLESEED

Attendance rates have not noticeably improved in the face of more than 100,000 filed cases. “Research indicates that overly punitive responses to truancy, including fines, exacerbate the problems that truancy alone creates. Additionally, court involvement, particularly for children who have had no previous experience with the criminal justice system, increases the likelihood of dropout,” Maura McInerney, legal director at the Education Law Center, stated during testimony at a legislative hearing on truancy on June 9, 2015. From the same report, Mary Schmid Mergler, director of Texas Appleseed’s School-to-Prison Pipeline Project, said in a press release, “In the vast majority of cases, the school, working with the student and family, could address the truancy problem if it made meaningful attempts to do so. Instead, schools often pass the responsibility to courts not designed, equipped, or trained to provide meaningful assistance to students and their families.” The glaring research shows that truancy court doesn’t improve outcomes. Parents, restorative practice, and juvenile justice advocates know this and are working to make their voices heard. Unfortunately, this awareness and knowledge is slow to reach our schools and presiding truancy court judges. The result is that too many schools are relying on old-school practices of punishing children with school avoidance and children absent for other reasons.

School Funding

Parents sometimes feel that their school only cares about their child’s attendance because it affects their district’s funding. While student attendance is a considerable factor contributing to funding, most educators genuinely care about their students and want them to succeed. No one wants to see a child fail or drop out of school.

However, financial consequences are attached to your child's attendance, which puts external pressure on your school administrators to get your child into school.

Across the United States, each state uses several funding models to count its K–12 students. Those calculations impact the allocation of dollars from state and local aid. Most recently, due to the increased chronic absenteeism post–COVID-19, state education departments are also implementing other incentives for improved attendance and, conversely, imposing actions and consequences for not improving attendance.

CHAPTER 11

Medication

Insights and Considerations

Medication may be one option for helping some school-avoidant children with mental health disorders. Because giving medication to children with mental health issues can be polarizing, it isn't always included in discussions and publications. However, this conversation is necessary. Medication can be integral to a child's recovery and, in some cases, save lives. Parents of children with anxiety, depression, OCD, and other mental health conditions must decide if they want to explore medication as part of their child's treatment. Most antidepressants available today have been used and studied for years, providing rich data and anecdotal information that doctors rely on to inform their prescribing decisions.

I sat down with Dr. Mona Potter, chief medical officer and co-founder of InStride Health, in hopes that she could provide a complete and balanced view to help guide this decision. Dr. Potter is a board-certified child and adolescent psychiatrist with two decades of clinical and administrative experience in the Harvard medical system. As the medical director of McLean Hospital's Child and Adolescent Outpatient Services, she co-developed several programs, including the McLean Anxiety Mastery Program (MAMP) and the McLean School Consultation Service. InStride Health is a leading provider in successfully treating children with school avoidance. Below are some highlights I took from my conversation with Dr. Potter.

Q: When should parents consider medication for their children?

A: There is research in the form of randomized controlled trials (RCT) on pediatric anxiety and OCD that can help with the medication decision. These studies look at the relative efficacy of what is considered to be gold standard medication (SSRI—selective serotonin reuptake inhibitor) vs. gold standard therapy (CBT—cognitive behavioral therapy) vs. placebo through four comparison groups: medication alone vs. medication + cognitive behavioral therapy (CBT) vs. CBT alone vs. placebo. The studies found that the combination of medication + CBT outperforms medication-only and CBT-only groups, which are about equal. All three intervention groups outperform placebo.

Based on these data and clinical experience, and because CBT can be so effective, the recommendation is typically to start with a trial of CBT for mild to moderate anxiety and/or OCD (assuming that CBT is available and the child is willing to engage; if not immediately available, it can be reasonable to consider a medication trial while waiting to access CBT). When the child presents with more moderate to severe symptoms, it can be helpful to consider a combination medication + CBT approach from the start. This approach acknowledges a biological, psychological, and social/ environmental aspect to the child's symptoms, and by addressing all parts, they are more likely to improve.

This is a personal decision that should be made with a trusted physician/prescriber.

Q: When would parents consider medication for children with school avoidance?

A: When considering medication for a child with school avoidance, start by considering the target of the medication. Medication will not target school-avoidance behavior, but it might help address underlying causes of school avoidance, such as anxiety, depression, and OCD.

For example, if a child's anxiety has started calling the shots in a way that's interfering with their life (e.g., leaving or skipping activities due to anxiety), that anxiety is changing the way that child is experiencing the world and learning from those experiences. Medication can help target the biological component of anxiety and turn down the intensity of the emotions to help make it feel more doable to talk back to the anxiety and approach the activities rather than avoid them.

Q: The conversation about giving children medication can be very polarizing. Some people are against it, while others eagerly seek it.

A: It is not unique to psychiatry to have a range of opinions about medications, though it is understandable that parents might feel hesitant to use medication to target their child's anxiety. Because most of us experience anxiety to some extent, it can feel challenging for parents to figure out where the threshold is for considering medication for their child's anxiety. It is important to have the conversation with a healthcare professional about the risks and benefits of the medication AND the risks and benefits of not taking medication. It is important to consider the impact the anxiety is having on the child's life and what potential harm comes by not tackling it with as many tools as needed for change. And if the anxiety is mild, then it is reasonable to start with therapy to see if that is enough. If not, then you know you have an additional tool that has been shown to be effective.

Q: How do you determine when a child is stable? How long do you keep them on medication?

A: When making decisions about how long to keep medication on board, child psychiatrists borrow from adult psychiatry literature and use clinical experience. The general expert consensus is to aim for a period of at least six months, but ideally twelve to eighteen months, during which the child is functioning (engaging in school and preferred activities, spending time with family and friends, etc.) AND feels they are in the emotional driver's seat (i.e., they feel their feelings, AND they made decisions based on their interests and values vs. fear and anxiety). After that six to eighteen months of stability, it is very reasonable to talk about a slow taper off of the medication. A slow taper allows new responses to anxiety to solidify. We want these responses to become a new behavioral pattern and see better success when we're patient with the taper process.

Q: Is relapse possible after tapering off medication?

A: Relapse is possible, so it is important to look for signs that the anxiety is getting stronger again—for example, starting to feel more over-whelmed by emotions or starting to make decisions in the context of emotions rather than values. Sometimes, it is enough to notice and name that the anxiety is ramping up, and at other times, it is an indication to do some booster sessions of treatment (and perhaps restart medication).

Q: How do you set realistic expectations for medications?

A: It's important to understand what medication can do and what it cannot do in order to know if it is working or not. Medication will not eliminate all of life's stressors or take away the emotions (we wouldn't want that—anxiety can be a helpful emotion at times!). Medication possibly can help decrease the intensity of the anxiety, which can help the child feel more able to approach anxiety-provoking situations rather than avoid them. Parents should make sure children are taking the medication as prescribed and giving it enough time to work. SSRIs can take twelve to twenty-four weeks for full effect, and the dose needs to be therapeutic.

Considerations

Dr. Potter aimed to provide this expert information from a balanced viewpoint in hopes it would inform and support parents in their decision-making process. Not only does Dr. Potter prescribe medications as a psychiatrist, but she also treats children who have school avoidance and mental health disorders. She understands the perspectives of our children with school avoidance as well as caregivers like you, so I greatly appreciated her insights and guidance. But as always, this interview was for informational purposes only and is not intended to replace medical advice from your physician—you should always have these discussions with your child's mental health professional.

Psychiatrists and other clinical medication prescribers like Dr. Potter determine which medications to use for a patient based on clinical research, their clinical judgment based on the client's symptoms, medical history, and feedback from their other patients.

Prescribing is not yet an exact science, so trial and error is required to find the proper treatment for an individual. Just because one medication didn't work doesn't mean another one will not. Clinicians monitor patients, which is a crucial component of medication management. Dosage is another important factor for parents to consider and keep on top of. If there is an unknown history of antidepressant medications for a child, doctors usually start at lower doses to monitor tolerability and side effects. So, parents should not be discouraged when a low dose of medication is not showing any therapeutic effects. The best practice is for doctors to taper up (increase dosage) according to a patient's tolerance and to elicit better results, as in a reduction of anxiety or depression.

The selective serotonin reuptake inhibitor (SSRI) class of antidepressants is usually the first line of treatment for depression and anxiety disorders. They have shown to be effective for a wide range of people: They help increase the serotonin levels in the brain, which can improve mood and reduce anxiety; generally have fewer and less severe side effects; are widely available in less expensive generic forms; and have been approved for treating panic disorder, OCD, PTSD, and social anxiety in addition to depression and other anxiety disorders.

Examples of SSRIs are (generic name first, brand name in parentheses):

- fluoxetine (Prozac)
- sertraline (Zoloft)
- citalopram (Celexa)
- escitalopram (Lexapro)
- paroxetine (Paxil)

When a patient has not responded to several SSRIs, clinicians often move to the SNRIs. SNRIs (serotonin-norepinephrine reuptake inhibitors) are often considered second-line treatments for depression and anxiety because they can have more side effects and may not be as well tolerated as SSRIs.

Common SNRIs:

- venlafaxine (Effexor)
- duloxetine (Cymbalta)
- desvenlafaxine (Pristiq)
- levomilnacipran (Fetzima)

SNRIs are commonly used to increase serotonin and norepinephrine levels in the brain. Norepinephrine is another neurotransmitter involved in regulating mood and stress responses. By blocking the reuptake of both serotonin and norepinephrine, SNRIs can help improve mood, increase energy levels, and reduce anxiety.

Pharmacogenetics (Genetic Testing)

You may have heard about the use of pharmacogenetics (genetic testing) in the last few years to help clinicians find the right medication for each individual.

Pharmacogenetic testing uses DNA to determine how your body metabolizes different antidepressants, which can influence their effectiveness and the likelihood of side effects. When you take an antidepressant (or almost any medication), it is metabolized by your liver enzymes. Some people are naturally fast metabolizers—meaning their liver enzymes break down drugs too quickly to be effective, and therefore they need higher doses to see results. Others are naturally slow metabolizers, which can result in a buildup of the drug in the body that could have potentially toxic side effects. To complicate matters, a person can be a "fast metabolizer" for some medications and a "slow metabolizer" for others, so it can be difficult to find the ideal medication and dosage.

Pharmacogenetic tests analyze key enzymes that metabolize antidepressants, antipsychotics, benzodiazepines, and other medications used for depression and anxiety treatment. This information helps doctors identify which medications might work better for you and which ones to avoid, ideally reducing the trial-and-error period often associated with finding the right antidepressant regimen.

Some pharmacogenetic tests will recommend one specific medication within a class (i.e., SSRI, SNRI), and some recommend just the class of medication and not the individual medication itself. The tests provide insights into how your body may respond to different medications. These tests can use saliva, a cheek swab, or blood. Because a cheek swab is so simple and noninvasive, it is the usual method for collecting DNA for these tests.

Psychiatrists have differing opinions on the benefits of pharmacogenetic testing. Some see it as a valuable tool for improving patient outcomes, potentially leading to faster recovery and fewer side effects. Some doctors note a possible placebo effect from receiving these recommendations, and some see better adherence to prescribed medication when parents and clients have more faith and hope in the effectiveness of the treatment.

Then, some practitioners remain skeptical due to the current lack of robust evidence, coupled with the costs associated with testing. Doctors often also fear the time lost in starting a medication while waiting for the results of the genetic tests to be delivered. Research continues to evolve as we seek more definitive guidance for finding the right medication for each individual.

CHAPTER 12

Alternative School Options

Exploring New Educational Paths for Success

As much as you may want to make it work for your child to stay at their current school, there are certainly instances where it may not be in your child's best interest to remain there.

However, it can be hard to know when it's time to stop pushing our children to attend school. Dr. Chris Kearney has addressed this common concern: "Part of it depends on the child's age. We push harder with elementary and early middle school children. High school is different because there are more learning-based options, and sometimes the problems are more chronic. There's no one-size-fits-all strategy, so I always explore options with families. Schools now offer better learning options than before. Consider hybrid learning, where students do part of the learning online and part in person while still accruing credits. There are many more nuanced options than there used to be."

Here are some reasons it might be time to explore other schooling options:

- You have worked with the school for months or even years, but they have not been willing or able to help your child effectively.
- Despite months or years of working with the school, your child still isn't making progress in attending school.
- Your child feels unsafe due to violence or bullying, and the school has not taken the necessary steps to correct the issue.
- The school environment isn't conducive to your child's well-being, perhaps due to overly rigorous academic or performance-based standards.
- You have tried everything you can and feel it is time to explore other options.

Making the decision to look for alternative school options is difficult, and it can feel intimidating to make such a significant change. As always, trust your judgment to do what is best for your child. If you're working with a therapist for yourself or your child, they can help guide you through this decision-making process as well.

A common concern is whether you can afford another school. You may assume private schools are your only option, which can be expensive. However, that's not always the case, so it's important to do your research first. You might qualify for an out-of-district placement, where the school district covers the cost of your child's education. (As a reminder: To pursue an out-of-district placement, your child typically needs an IEP, not just a 504. This is another reason to aim for an IEP if your child qualifies for both.) It's advisable to consult with a special education attorney if you're considering an out-of-district placement to ensure that you're following the correct procedures and safeguarding your child's chances of qualification.

There are more choices available these days, especially after the COVID-19 pandemic highlighted the need for alternative options. Mental health professionals who treat children with school avoidance used to take a hard line against removing children from in-person schooling, but they have since adjusted their advice and recommendations on an individual basis.

Alternatives within Your School District

Before looking outside the district for another school, consider that some districts offer alternative schooling options that may be appropriate and helpful for your child. One beneficial practice gaining traction is the creation of alternative school programs within districts, either developed by the district itself or managed by an external organization, which cater to individual student needs.

Alternative School Programs Built by Your School District

These programs may be entire school programs located in separate buildings or setups that have your child move between buildings on campus. This way, your child might attend some classes (or just counseling and individualized support) in one building while taking their regular or special education classes in the main school building. While these programs should be listed on your district's website, they may not be, so always ask.

School Programs Run by External (Third-Party) Companies or Organizations

In some cases, your school district may hire an outside company to run supplemental or therapeutic programs in district buildings. These programs often provide individual and group therapy, and sometimes academic support. Ideally, the program would have a designated case manager or coach to manage your child's progress across both the program and the regular school, ensuring that there is coordination with teachers and staff. Examples of such programs include Effective School Solutions (ESS) and the Brookline Resilient Youth Team (BRYT), available in several states.

Some of these external programs are expensive, charged on a per-student basis, which may incentivize the district to return your child to regular schooling quickly. In contrast, district-run programs often have fixed costs for staff, buildings, and curriculum, so keeping your child in such a program doesn't add additional expenses.

Both types of programs are often considered transitional. Once your child improves and is no longer school-avoidant, they may return to their original school. Make sure this transition is gradual, using reintegration or exposure methods to ease the move.

Independent Specialized Education Schools

Independent specialized education schools, either day or boarding, cater to students with specific learning disabilities such as dyslexia, ADHD, executive functioning challenges, or autism. These schools focus on students whose weak language skills impede comprehension and communication, key components of school success.

Therapeutic Day Schools

Therapeutic day schools integrate therapy into the school structure, providing individual and group therapy, and sometimes a family therapy component. Class sizes are small, and adult support is high. Each child may have a dedicated advisor or coach who serves as their advocate, coordinating between teachers, clinicians, and families to ensure that the student receives necessary support.

Therapeutic Boarding Schools

Therapeutic boarding schools offer the same support as day schools, but the child lives on campus. These schools can be helpful for school-avoidant children, providing structure and support to get the child to attend daily when parents have been unsuccessful. They can also be an option for children who have retreated into their bedrooms and refuse to leave. Like day schools, these institutions offer a dedicated advisor or coach who works with the child regularly.

When considering a program, ensure that your child fits the student profile, usually found in the admissions section of the school's website. Some schools focus more on behavioral problems, which may not be the right environment for a school-avoidant child.

In some cases, if your child's functioning has been significantly compromised, a treatment program may be necessary before attending a therapeutic day or boarding school (see higher levels of care in Chapter 2).

Small Private Schools

Small private schools offer more intimate class sizes (three to twelve students) and individualized attention, which can be beneficial for children who need a quieter and more personalized learning environment. While these schools don't receive federal funding and aren't required to follow Child Find, Section 504, or IDEA guidelines, they often provide their own versions of individualized education plans.

Democratic or Self-Directed Schools

These schools vary widely in structure and philosophy, but their core concept is that students have more freedom in their education, often integrating hands-on learning and using nontraditional evaluation methods.

Online Schools

Many families with school-avoidant children move to online schools because they feel they have no other option. However, some school districts are quick to give up on these kids and intentionally suggest that students move to an online option.

The number of online schools has grown tremendously since COVID-19. Many states now have their own online charter schools that are public schools at no cost to you. Check your state's Department of Education website to see what your state offers.

The conundrum of online school for school-avoidant students is that most of our kids don't fit the profile of what it takes for a student to thrive online.

For example, Learning Lab provides the following criteria to determine if online schooling fits a child.

Online school is best for students who

- are self-motivated,
- are traditional learners (no learning disabilities or large subject weaknesses),
- are self-advocates,
- are able to stick to a structured schedule they create or that is provided by the parent, and
- have strong executive functioning skills.

You may be reading this list and thinking that your child does not fit an online student profile, and many of you are right. So, yes, this is the dilemma. Most children who go to online schooling don't fit that profile, and the same is true for school-avoidant children.

Online schools also have a school-avoidance problem, so they are realizing that most of their student population doesn't meet the traditional online student criteria. Because of this, many of them are looking for ways to better engage with students and families and meet the needs of their school-avoidant students, who make up a subsection of their enrollment.

When determining the suitability of an online school for your child, you must be diligent in asking how it is different from other schools in terms of how it reintegrates and reengages school-avoidant students. Again, every child is different, and you know your child best when determining if an online education would work for them.

Homeschooling

Homeschooling is the education of a child at home, with the parents taking full responsibility for the child's education and associated costs. Families may follow a specific homeschool curriculum or create their own.

Unschooling

Unschooling is considered a version of homeschooling, but it may not be done in the home or follow a set curriculum. "Unschooling is a broad term that encompasses a range of labels, definitions, and practices unique to each person or family. At its core, it's the opportunity for children to explore their own interests rather than adhere to the criteria and curricula predetermined by school boards or other entities. Unlike the traditional homeschool model which often seeks to mimic the classroom or follow a defined curriculum usually with parents acting as teachers, in unschooling, children take the lead. Adults, sometimes (but not always) parents, typically offer support, assistance, and guidance when needed."

Unschooling, emphasizing how natural curiosity can lead to effective learning without traditional schooling structures, can look different from family to family.

Through feedback from families in the School Avoidance Alliance, it's clear that no one-size-fits-all answer exists when deciding between online schooling, homeschooling, or unschooling. Trust your judgment, as you know your child better than anyone.

The Experts Weigh In

Child psychologists have changed their perspectives on online schooling, homeschooling, and unschooling due to the increasing number of children who struggle in traditional school settings. While many previously insisted that school-avoidant children should return to brick-and-mortar schools, some now recognize that traditional schools are not suitable for every child.

Dr. Tammy Moscrip, executive director and chief administrator at The Spire School, holds a doctorate in psychology and specializes in working with children and families. The Spire School, located in Stamford, Connecticut, is a state-approved special education program and independent, therapeutic day school for intellectually capable students in grades 8–12 who are struggling academically and emotionally. Many school-avoidant children have found success there.

Q: Do you have an opinion about online schooling for school-avoidant children?

A: Dr. Moscrip: When we found out the world was shutting down in March 2020, we were ready to roll with a synchronous, fully online program for nine periods a day. At first, we were so excited; students were sitting in bed with their pajamas, logged on, and we were like "Wow. Why didn't we think of this? We should have had a hybrid program all along." And then, a month went by, and the novelty wore off. And then, we found increased disengagement, and absenteeism, and decreased productivity, communication, and certainly socialization.

For our students, it has a different level of engagement, accountability, and enthusiasm as a learning center. We have found that time and again, something is missing about the relationships, the physical proximity, and the ability to spontaneously interact. Online learning has its time and place, and some students can thrive if they have strong executive function skills, are very conscientious and intrinsically motivated, and have a goal and will stick to it. For most of our students, it wore out its welcome quickly and was socially isolating.

Dr. Chris Kearney, whom you met in Chapter 1, is a leading researcher on school avoidance, author, and professor at the University of Nevada, Las Vegas. He is also the director of the UNLV Child School Refusal and Anxiety Disorders Clinic. He is one of the foremost researchers in the field of school avoidance and is the creator of the Four Functions of School Refusal and the School Refusal Assessment Scale (SRAS).

Q: Do you have opinions or guidance you can share about online education, unschooling, or home-based learning? Parents are defaulting to alternative school options because they feel their school cannot accommodate their child. Do you have any opinions, guidance, or ideas about this?

A: Dr. Kearney: Yes, there are a lot more choices for public, in-person schooling than there ever used to be. And if it fits within a family's value system, I don't have a problem with it. If a child goes through homeschooling or has homebound instruction because of some medical condition, there's a variety of other formats now that are out there—post-pandemic hybrid formats and distance learning and remote formats, all kinds of things we have at the university level as well. It's a huge mindset shift in the post-pandemic era.

The only time I issue a warning about that is when homebound instruction is explicitly used as an avoidance strategy for the school. So, if the idea is, we're going to place the child in some kind of homebound instruction format now because their anxiety is high, and later, we're going to try to get them back into an in-person school, that doesn't usually work. If you aim to get them back into a regular classroom setting, it's better to do that now instead of waiting several months, because you're making the problem slightly more challenging to solve. Other than that, I respect that families have different preferences when educating their children.

You must remember that if kids learn online, they do everything else in their lives online. So, you can have a teenager doing online learning, but if they go out with their friends and they're doing neighborhood things or clubs or groups or sports that are in person and they're developing those social interpersonal skills, that's okay. It's only when kids are in their room twenty-four hours a day and are not socializing with anybody that that kind of isolation can be harmful.

Parent Perspectives: Navigating Alternative Schooling Options

Many school-avoidance families feel uncertain about trying alternative schooling options, which is completely understandable. You love your child and just want the best for them.

Through conversations with thousands of families, I've learned that trying an alternative schooling option doesn't have to be a final, permanent decision. Families often move between schooling options. These transitions don't typically "break" children; rather, they provide insights into what works and what doesn't for their child.

Some families find that after a period of online schooling or homeschooling, their children return to traditional schools. Others try several options before settling on what's best for their child. Here are some firsthand experiences from parents who have tried alternative schooling options.

Parent 1

"We've been homeschooling my sixteen-year-old daughter. It's been worth it for her mental health! One day at a time. She still has social anxiety, but we've been working through it. We go grocery shopping, and she comes with me to the gym, even if she doesn't work out."

Parent 2

"I can't say enough about unschooling. It has worked wonders for our son. After a period of doing nothing, we got him a tutor, and now he's engaged and talking about going to college."

Parent 3

"Homeschooling didn't work for my ADHD/anxiety child. We tried unschooling, which was better for peace in the house, but my older child dropped into a depression and couldn't leave the bedroom."

Parent 4

"We homeschooled for part of second grade and switched to a new school for third. My child did much better and is starting fourth grade now."

Parent 5

"We unschooled in ninth grade, and after a year and a half, my son enrolled in GED classes at a local college. Public K–12 just wasn't for him."

Parent 6

"My sixth-grader did an online charter for a year to adjust therapy and meds. He's now back to in-person school, and so far, it's going well."

Parent 7

"My son did online school for grades 7–9 and returned to in-person last year. While he still had absences, he attended more regularly and did better."

Parent 8

"We've gone back and forth between homeschooling and public school for years. He's starting ninth grade now, and we're hoping he can complete the year."

Parent 9

"After a year of homeschooling, my daughter returned to her regular school. We've had some hiccups, but overall, she's going 85 percent of the time."

Parent 10

"My son did online school for part of fifth grade and is excited to start public school for sixth. We're hoping the structure helps him stay engaged."

Parent 11

"We pulled our children from private school and homeschooled them for a few months. Now they're enrolled in public school, and they're excited for the change."

Parent 12

"My oldest child moved from public school to being unschooled at the end of his sophomore year in high school. He dual-enrolled in community college, which initially went well. Then he got COVID and fell too far behind. He continued unschooling and graduated in June. He's now enrolled in the engineering program at our community college. Yesterday, he went on his own and completed his class work. He wants to transfer to a university next year.

Our youngest, who had only a little avoidance, wanted to homeschool, too. He's highly involved in a local art program and is taking a full load through dual enrollment at the community college. I hope the youngest will help the oldest not sit in his car between classes on the days they're on campus together.

Letting both follow their paths helped them focus on themselves, their well-being, and their future. It was the best option for us. They both have future plans and can see that there is a future, and I think that's amazing."

Parent 13

"My son attended public school for kindergarten, homeschooled for first grade, and went back to public school for second. I pulled him out in third grade and homeschooled him for six years. He went back to school two years ago and is doing well. It's not easy—I think school will never be as easy for him as it is for most kids—but he managed to make some friends (even if they're just school friends, not out-of-school friends). Academically, he's doing okay. He missed a lot of school over the last two years, but his IEP helps with that a bit. It's still a struggle to get him to go most days, but I've got my fingers crossed for this year."

Parent 14

"Our child completed the last quarter of last year online, which was a great choice for us at the time. He's starting back in person next month, but we're open to pivoting back to online if needed."

Parent 15

"We eventually decided to homeschool my son while he was being treated for PANS. [Pediatric acute-onset neuropsychiatric syndrome (PANS) is a clinical diagnosis given to children who experience a dramatic, sometimes overnight onset of neuropsychiatric symptoms, including obsessions, compulsions, or food restrictions.] That was the best decision ever. The stress over school was unbearable, and he wasn't learning anything anyway. We focused on educational material that interested him. But, of course, research your state's law first."

Parent 16

"My son is in sixth grade and has been in a fully remote charter school since third grade. It's been a better fit for him than brick-and-mortar schools ever were. He's attending North Carolina Cyber Academy now, which offers different engagement tiers based on the student's needs. Some classes are flexible (asynchronous), while others are traditional (synchronous). For example, my son's math class is compacted—he took sixth-grade math in the first semester and seventh-grade math in the second. He decides each morning whether he needs extra support by attending the live class or working independently. His teachers have been great. His science and social studies teacher even schedules individual sessions with him as needed. The live ELA (English Language Arts) class lets him practice peer interactions, and he also attends an IEP support session weekly. Overall, it's been a good fit for him, and we even get quarterly consults with an occupational therapist (OT) for fine motor and executive functioning support."

Parent 17

"I took my daughter out of public school and enrolled her in a private online school to finish high school. I struggled with this decision for a long time. Initially, I avoided online options because of how it went during COVID, and I wanted her to be around people to develop social skills.

"But in March 2023, she completely shut down, and I couldn't get her back to school despite having her on an IEP, in counseling, and on medication. She finished the year with Hospital Homebound instruction to preserve all her hard work. I tried to make public school work for her, but it became clear it wasn't the right environment. Her mental health is my top priority, and now she's much happier. While I know there will still be struggles to keep her motivated and to help her build social skills, I'm hopeful this will allow her to graduate without the stress of getting to school every day."

Parent 18

"We homeschooled for three-quarters of a year—the best decision ever. At the time, I thought my daughter would finish school this way, but she successfully transitioned to a private high school afterward! Sometimes these kids just need to see that they have options. Knowing that is often enough to help them move forward."

Parent 19

"Our son attends a virtual charter school that offers both synchronous and asynchronous classes. We left public school in October, and he made the honor roll at his new school for the rest of the year. He logs in at 8:30 a.m., but he has until the end of the week to complete his work. He can wake up, log in, and go back to sleep or have a relaxed morning. We've made him choose two activities to get him out of the house (and we won't have to worry about truancy court if he misses those occasionally). I work from home most days, and helping him with his schoolwork has helped us identify where his anxiety around school and social interaction comes from. It's also taught us a lot about how he learns, which has helped us create a good work schedule."

Parent 20

"We weren't happy with online school during COVID, so we were reluctant to consider it again. But after trying public school multiple times, we realized it wasn't going to work. We researched alternatives and found an online program that has been a great fit, and has melted away a lot of my daughter's anxiety. She still struggles with anxiety, but without the daily overwhelm, she's been able to work on coping skills and thrive in areas where she's strong. She's applied for a job, had an interview, and is now participating in a school open house online with her IEP team. Progress can be slow, but it happens. Stick with them—most kids don't want to feel 'different' and need understanding."

Parent 21 (Me, Jayne)

During my son's years of school avoidance, we met with many psychologists and psychiatrists. I remember one therapist suggesting we consider a private school, as his public school might not be the right fit. I was adamantly opposed, mainly due to fears about the tuition costs. This was around 2009, and there weren't many alternative options then. A year or two later, my son's psychiatrist recommended we look into boarding schools. I cried uncontrollably at the thought of him leaving home. But several months later, as his bedroom became his cocoon of safety and isolation, his condition worsened.

We decided to send him to a treatment program (Rogers Behavioral Health in Wisconsin) that specialized in anxiety disorders, school avoidance, and OCD's. After treatment, his psychiatrist strongly advised us to send him to a therapeutic boarding school. We followed his advice, and my son thrived at the Grove School in Connecticut, eventually moving to a small, nontherapeutic boarding school (the Darrow School in New York), where he graduated. I'm grateful for both schools, as they allowed my son to finish his education, enjoy his last few years of high school, and go on to college.

Our story, as well as the above experiences of other families, show that the decision to try alternative school options varies from child to child and family to family. Remember that you may try a different program or approach, and if it's not a good fit, you can always return to where your child started. Some children improve after a reprieve from the current situation that isn't working for them, and then return successfully to in-person learning with fewer challenges than before.

CHAPTER 13

Parent Success Stories

Valuable Advice from the Trenches

Parents of children with school avoidance are constantly looking for ways to help their child. The knowledge and guidance gained from our experts is invaluable—but hearing about the experiences and successes of other parents in a similar situation adds a whole new layer of empowerment.

When I was navigating school avoidance with my son, I was desperate to connect with other families. I wanted to know what worked for them, what didn't, and what to watch out for. Most of all, I needed *hope*.

As families dealing with school avoidance, we know that this is a different animal. It's misunderstood, isolating, stigmatizing, and downright scary. It also requires a determined and resourceful caregiver to gather the information needed to get your child the support they need and deserve.

Since starting the School Avoidance Alliance in 2014, I have connected with and spoken to thousands of families dealing with this issue. Like you, they are strong, smart, and fiercely dedicated to their children.

When these families discover solutions that have helped their children return to school, they love to share them with others in similar situations. And through this book, they'd now like to share their stories of their paths through school avoidance with you.

Their stories are rich in information, guidance, and advice—and they can provide lots of hope. I know you'll take away valuable lessons that will help you and your child.

Parent Story 1, by M.N.

Q: Could you start by sharing some brief information about your child to help other families see how your situation might relate to theirs?

A: My son, J, has ADHD, anxiety, and depression. He struggles to be in public and spends a lot of time in his room. Even when he found the perfect school, he didn't hang out with those friends outside of school. He thinks he is smarter than most people and needs to be challenged. He does have a big heart and is a funny kid, but he doesn't show as much of that side of himself anymore.

My daughter, M, has severe anxiety, ADHD, frontal lobe and executive functioning deficit, and a working memory deficit. She is a bubbly kid who has a lot of friends. She hides her emotions well for the most part. Her teachers have always thought she was a joy. Then she comes home and takes it all out on me. Sometimes I think she used up all her "good" at school. In the morning, if she wakes up for school, it doesn't necessarily mean she will go to school.

Sometimes she will get all ready and then start crying and say she just can't do it and crawl back in bed. She says she wants to go to school and she wants to see her friends, but she just can't. Bribing and punishment don't work. Sometimes I can coax her out of the house and to school and she will stay all day, and sometimes she just can't do it.

Q: What therapy worked and what didn't?

A: J was going to counseling with a therapist he liked, and it was working really well. But that therapist moved, and we had trouble finding another good fit. The right therapy for your individual child can make all the difference. He started going to neurofeedback [a type of mind-body therapy that detects brain waves and affects brain activity] for about five months and I believe that made a difference in his anxiety. He was able to be in more social situations and started speaking up in school more.

M's school avoidance began at the end of eighth grade. She has always had severe anxiety, so we thought the schoolwork was just getting harder. After completing a neuropsych evaluation, we discovered it was a lot more than that. When she started ninth grade, we got an IEP in place, and she had much more support. She had a school counselor she trusted and that made a difference, but she would leave class frequently and just go sit in the counselor's office. She missed 25 percent of the days of her freshman year.

Although my daughter missed a lot of school, I believe the neurofeedback and the right medications for anxiety are what got her there most days. Plus sleep was a huge issue. When we started addressing the sleep component in her neurofeedback therapy, she started sleeping better and it made everything better.

M will be a sophomore next year. She had a private therapist and it helped, but they never made much progress together. About seven months ago, we started going to family therapy and talked a lot about school avoidance. It seemed like everything always came back to that. It was a common ground where we could get out our frustrations and come up with strategies to try. Some worked and some didn't, but we always went back and talked it through. It was very healing for our relationship. School avoidance is a huge strain on the family structure. Especially as a single mom who has them half time and takes the brunt of it; it was exhausting.

Q: Did your child try any programs or treatments (intensive outpatient, partial, inpatient) that helped them make progress? If so, what aspects helped your child?

A: J was a risk to himself (not school related), so we took him to the hospital to be evaluated. They admitted him to the psych ward. He spent a week there in denial that anything was wrong. He was very angry with us and blamed us for putting him there. This all happened right at the end of the sophomore school year. Getting him to summer school was a huge struggle. He actually hadn't missed a lot of school because of avoidance; he just wouldn't do the work. At the start of junior year he went to school every day but sat in the bathroom ALL DAY. The school team reworked his IEP and gave him lots of options, but nothing worked. The alternative school in our town would have been great, but they were booked until the end of the school year. The school suggested partial hospitalization, but there was no way he was going back to that place, and ultimately it would just be a temporary fix.

Q: Do (or did) you utilize an alternative school to help your child get back to learning?

A: After the school suggested partial hospitalization for J, I started frantically researching for other options. I found a small, alternative, private school in our town called Learning with Meaning.

Learning with Meaning was founded by a mom who was struggling with her son and didn't know where else to turn. It began as a homeschool program and developed into an accredited school. There are thirty kids total enrolled in middle-high school. Around fifteen to twenty attend daily. Some kids attend online or only take some classes at the school.

I am beyond blessed to have found this school, and I believe it is the reason my son is still alive today.

J learned a ton there, but he still wasn't able to turn things in, even with the handholding. He was very far behind because of not doing schoolwork for a year or two, and didn't have all the credits to graduate as school was coming to an end. We let J "graduate," but I am still not sure when he will actually get a diploma. Getting him motivated is still a struggle. He is also working with vocational rehabilitation for his education/career.

Q: Did you make any changes to your home environment, parenting approach, actions, or communication style that helped your child?

A: My kids are very different and responded very differently to interventions. My son just needed to get out of the school—there was no way things were going to change if he stayed, and he was starting to experiment with drinking and drugs. The change in the school made all the difference. I could go on and on about what that school did for him. Toward the end of his senior year, he was done and didn't want to go, but that was the case for most kids his age. I think it is important to remember that there are times when avoiding school isn't so atypical.

With M, the biggest change was communication, which is something we figured out in family therapy. We came up with a plan and had open communication when one of us was not following the plan. Most of our conflicts happened because she wouldn't go to school and I needed to go to work. So if she wasn't ready, it made me late for work. I would sometimes have to find rides for her at lunch because she would decide she was ready to go. There was a lot of yelling and cruelty until we started therapy.

Q: What accommodations, modifications, or services from your school are helping (or helped) you make progress?

A: For M, we changed her first period to a study skills class so if she was late it wasn't such a big deal. The school did not penalize her for being late, but she was encouraged to be there on time. She almost never was. But in the beginning, if she was going to be late, she wouldn't go at all. After the school worked with us, she started being able to go late during first period, or even at lunch. But she also sometimes called to be picked up from school—that was harder to resolve.

In public school, both my kids had what they call a "laminate pink slip," which was basically a "get out of class any time" pass. They could just flash that pass and leave the room. The idea was that they could go get help, or take a break and go right back. This didn't work for my son, but it was a lifesaver for my daughter.

I think one of the most helpful things for my daughter, M, was attending her IEP. She has a simplified list of her IEP accommodations that she keeps with her, which helped her understand what she was entitled to. She felt like she could speak up about certain things because she knew what she could ask for. I think it feels empowering to her. Being able to hold the teachers accountable is huge.

One big anxiety provoker for M was knowing when her classes were. She put her class schedule on her phone screen saver so she could quickly glance at it. The school also allowed her to be in classes with friends to help with anxiety, and she could always pick her seat. She preferred to sit away from the door with her back to the wall so she could see the whole room.

In public school, those types of accommodations didn't help my son. The main positive changes at his private school that helped were:

- Smaller class sizes.
- Only two classes a day as opposed to seven (so less transition).
- Field trips, lots of hands-on learning, and weekly hikes.
- A relaxed atmosphere with places to chill out.
- A mixed age group so they could all help each other.
- No tests (for the most part). They had to do some assignments and show they had mastery over the subject at the end of the class.
- The students had some ownership over their education and environment. The students helped run the school—they had committees—and cleaned the school every Friday. And they were able to choose to take classes that interested them.

All schools work differently, and the way you approach every school ends up looking different. Parents need to make sure they know their rights and have advocates when necessary. Looking into your office of public instruction and your state's parent training information center is helpful. Here in Montana, that is the Montana Empowerment Center. I have called them many times, and I refer to them when I see families in my office struggling with the school system.

Q: If you are homeschooling, what is working and what are the challenges?

A: I could never homeschool my children. Their motivation and my patience work against us. Doing it during COVID was enough for a lifetime. I just need the schools to be more open-minded to alternative learning.

Q: What helped you get what you needed from the school to help your child?

A: I don't think the school helped much at all. The advantage my kids had was my career, connections, and my experience working with IEP teams in the past. I feel horrible for parents that don't know their rights or who they can go to for support. This is such an isolating position to be in. I have one friend with a son the same age as mine (we met when they were five), and we became our own support system. We talked about how to deal with our specific school system and what was working and not working. Both of our kids also attended neurofeedback therapy.

M got what she needed because she finally found her voice and started speaking up. She became more confident and advocated for herself. We didn't know she had it in her, but I truly think the neurofeedback is helping.

I also called the Montana Empowerment Center when I didn't know something. Their guidance always helped me to approach the school with a calm presence (when I could), and knowing my rights was helpful.

Q: What advice do you wish you had known earlier?

A: I wish I had realized this was out of their [my kids'] control and not a choice they were making. I also want others to know that the school system is not set up for neurodiverse learners. We need to find a way to change how they are teaching our kids. We need to start thinking outside the box and making learning fun and engaging. Look in your community for schools that fit your child's needs. The school I found for my son was a great fit for him, but wouldn't be the answer for some people because every kid learns differently. Don't give up. Find a support system and see a therapist yourself. Family therapy was also a lifesaver for our relationship.

Q: Do you have any thoughts or experiences you'd like to share about medications that were helpful for your child?

A: My children are on anxiety meds and have an as-needed anxiety med. The as-needed is very helpful, but if they are too escalated, they will have to come home anyway and then take it.

Q: Do you have any words of hope or encouragement for families who may be struggling right now?

A: This is not on you. Take it easy on yourself, walk away when you can, and remember this won't last forever. Whatever path your child takes to get through school is not as important as their mental health.

Parent Story 2, by C.H.

Q: Could you start by sharing some brief information about your child to help other families see how your situation might relate to theirs?

A: My son's issues with school started in grade school. While he had friends, he was shy and sometimes withdrawn. He had a very hard time joining group activities. Sometimes he would melt down after school. Over the grade school years, there would be periods of time where everything seemed fine; however, there were also times he resisted going to school or would shut down at school. He would often run out of steam over the course of the academic year. He would begin the year doing all his work, a bright student doing very well, and eventually disengage. After a couple of "good years," things became difficult in seventh grade. It started with isolated issues, like attending gym class, and developed into "I can't go."

The school was supportive. Honestly, I still do not know the source of the school avoidance. It may have been social anxiety and/or may have been temperament or neurodivergence. When he started therapy in grade school, his therapist suggested a change in school environment. In retrospect, I wish I had moved him to a smaller, more progressive school at that time. I thought things would get better—and sometimes they were better—and I was worried about expenses. However, I think he would have done better in a different environment—and changing schools is a much bigger deal as a teenager than as a grade school student. I also wish the school had assessed the neurodivergent issue beyond "Does your child line up their toys?"

Q: What therapy worked and what didn't?

A: Prior to switching to online school in tenth grade and before the pandemic, we had moderate to good improvement with a combination of CBT, an SSRI, and a gradual exposure plan developed on a weekly basis with a therapist. The therapist was in communication with the school and shared the weekly plan, which addressed the attendance concerns. The plan increased attendance in very small increments, and only after a week of adhering to the previous plan. There was a lot of positive reinforcement and mutually agreed upon rewards such as cell phone use. At the onset of the pandemic, my son was attending most classes on most days. At the same time, it required a great deal of flexibility with my work to attend sessions and transport him to and from school. I knew it was not a long-term solution for us without more consistency with attendance. Also, even with the improved attendance, things were still challenging in terms of keeping up with academic work. We ended this therapy at the onset of the pandemic and decided not to repeat it when attendance was a challenge after the pandemic.

Q: Did you make any changes to your home environment, parenting approach, actions, or communication style that helped your child?

A: It was helpful to receive therapeutic support to help me formulate a plan for each morning, so I did not react emotionally to the situation.

Q: What accommodations, modifications, or services from your school are helping (or helped) you make progress?

A: The school was able to modify academic expectations and grading in middle school, which took some pressure off. They also communicated with the therapist to receive a weekly attendance plan.

Q: Do you want to share anything about any intervention plan, 504, or IEP for your child? What aspects helped and what was not helpful in them?

A: The 504 and IEP were always a step behind what was going on and were only moderately helpful.

Q: If you are homeschooling, what is working and what are the challenges?

A: We did not homeschool, but considered it a viable option.

Q: If your child is doing online school, is it working? Why do you think it worked or didn't work for your child?

A: My son started at a public online school at the beginning of tenth grade when attendance remained an issue after the pandemic and starting high school. It worked out very well! He graduated and was accepted to all three colleges he applied to. It was a difficult decision and we considered all the options. I think online worked for him because he had good academic skills, he was old enough to be at home alone, and I had a partly remote schedule and was able to support the transition.

Online school took a lot of pressure off and allowed him to undertake more flexible exposures to social situations. I think he is able to cope much better simply due to maturity and having a break from 7:30 a.m.–3:00 p.m. schooling. His mood improved quickly after the transition, and he began taking music lessons. He also started working (very) part-time in our community a few months later. He studied for the ACT, took it, and did well.

When he first started studying online, I was very involved in supporting his schedule and work, but was completely hands-off by his last year. The school we chose was very supportive and flexible and offered a wide range of classes. It was a difficult decision, but we had to try something new. I do not think he would have been well-served by our continuing to try to make things work at his old school.

Q: What advice do you wish you had known earlier?

A: The most helpful part of our difficult journey was connecting with other families who had been in similar situations. When it started, I was completely overwhelmed. After I was connected with a number of people through friends and neighbors, I realized we were not alone. I also learned that there are many options for working through school avoidance. Everyone had tried different things and everyone had come through it in a better place. This provided a lot of emotional support and gave us more confidence in making decisions.

Q: Do you have any thoughts or experiences you'd like to share about medications that were helpful for your child?

A: Prozac was helpful for him.

Q: Do you have any words of hope or encouragement for families who may be struggling right now?

A: It can get better. This isn't happening because of anything you did or didn't do. Chances are, nobody knows why it is happening. A lot of people have been through it and know how hard it is. Take care of yourself. Talk to as many people as you can to identify your options and do what feels right for you and your family.

Parent Story 3, by J.G.

Q: Could you start by sharing some brief information about your child to help other families see how your situation might relate to theirs?

A: My daughter is currently seventeen and her school avoidance started in October 2022, her junior year of high school. She just graduated in June. We are from Long Island, New York.

Q: What therapy worked and what didn't?

A: My daughter did not react well at all to more punitive-based therapy (aka "tough love"). We tried a six-week school-avoidance program through our local healthcare system (recommended by her school) in which they wanted to do exposure therapy (driving to the school, even if she didn't go in, etc.), but they also wanted us to make her uncomfortable at home and deny her things.

For instance, she enjoys going on long walks (which I think is good for her mental health), but the therapists wanted her to "earn" those walks by going to school first. They also didn't want us to allow her to get her driver's license or drive ("that's a privilege") or to allow her to work ("school is her job first"). Our daughter stopped going to the program about halfway through, and we did not agree to deprive her of these things, because we did not think it would be helpful for her. In fact, we thought those suggestions would make her mental health worse! The program was not happy with us, but I have no regrets at refusing their techniques. I feel my daughter knew we listened to her, and I don't think what they were suggesting would have any impact on getting her to school, since much of her avoidance was based on trauma-induced anxiety.

What *did* help was the alternative high school (a pilot program through our school district) that she attended for her senior year, which placed a big emphasis on students' mental health and treating them as a whole person. The social workers and teachers there were extremely compassionate and bent over backward to try to meet her where she was. She had erratic attendance her final year, but she did attend a lot more and managed to graduate. *This* is how you help kids who are struggling: not taking away all of their will to live by "punishing" them and making them "uncomfortable while at home."

I found this especially true because my daughter was the victim of a sexual assault a few years back. I absolutely refused to punish her even more than she had been; I'm still shocked the school-avoidance program completely disregarded that part of the equation. They were solely interested in getting her into school full-time by the end of the six-week program; for any other help she needed, they suggested she attend outside therapy (which we agreed/agree she still needs, but their techniques were not helpful in the interim).

Q: Did your child try any programs or treatments (intensive outpatient, partial program, inpatient) that helped them make progress?

A: No, no program like that. She did go to traditional talk therapy twice (once for about a year, and then for another six months). She did not like therapy and has since refused to go back (she thinks it won't ever help), though we would like her to once we find a therapist she clicks with. We're hoping to eventually get her back in, and she has cracked the door a little recently on that possibility.

Q: Did you make any changes to your home environment, parenting approach, actions, or communication style that helped your child?

A: Only after joining the School Avoidance FB group did we make headway at home. I completely shifted gears at that point and parented with more compassion (I wasn't *not* compassionate before, but there was a lot more wheedling, crying, arguing, and pleading with her to go to school). We let her set her own pace and attend school when she felt comfortable (which was only doable because the school worked with us). We didn't "punish" her on the days she didn't go in, though she did have to hand over her phone during school hours (she got it back at 2:30 p.m.), had to get up at a reasonable hour (by 10 a.m. or so), and had to do something productive, whether it was schoolwork at home, helping me around the house, cleaning her room, working on community service stuff, or even watching educational videos or movies—all stuff she could do at her own pace, and she made the choice on what she wanted to do (I gave her various acceptable options, and she chose from those options). I didn't want her to idle in bed all day, which I feared would make the depression she also suffered from worse, so I tried to come up with a happy medium.

Q: What accommodations, modifications, or services from your school are helping (or helped) you make progress?

A: Her high school did make IEP/504 accommodations, though that wasn't enough to keep her in school. At the time, the accommodations included allowing her to leave class to sit in the calmer student lounge or in the social worker's office (she was a very nice, caring woman, so that was somewhat helpful) though my daughter rarely took advantage of the opportunities to leave class, as her social anxiety kept her anxious about kids noticing her leaving all the time. Her accommodations also included extra time on some assignments. The school also wiped out one full quarter of nonattendance from her record for medical reasons, replacing failing grades with no grades at all so it wouldn't affect her GPA. This was very helpful in her worst quarter so that she was still able to graduate with a high-80s GPA.

When all of that still wasn't getting her into school much more, the high school recommended she attend her senior year at the new alternative high school in our district, which was the key in helping her graduate. It was held in an off-site building in town, with only about a dozen kids grades 9–12, as well as teachers who came over from the high school.

In the alternative high school, they tried to give minimal, if any, homework, so that she could complete all her work in school with the assistance of her teachers. That helped *tremendously.* (Of course, we don't know how well she's going to do in her first semester of college, which she wants to try to attend; she hasn't been accustomed to doing work at home for at least two years.)

Q: Do you want to share anything about any intervention plan, 504, or IEP for your child? What aspects helped and what was not helpful in them?

A: I don't really feel the IEP/504 plans helped us that much.

Q: If your child is doing online school, is it working? Why do you think it worked or didn't work for your child?

A: For the most part, we didn't do online school, though for one semester in her junior year, she did online tutoring at the school's recommendation. This did not work well for us, since each class was just once a week and she needed help in the periods between the classes to complete homework.

Q: What helped you get what you needed from the school to help your child?

A: She had an absolutely amazing guidance counselor who helped us navigate everything for the past two years and served as a buffer for us for a lot. We would not have been able to get through this without him or the folks at the alternative high school. The common denominator with all of these helpful people that made all the difference with our daughter? Compassion, positivity, gentle nudging—not punitive "tough love" or threats.

Q: Your specific advice, based on your personal experience, could be a beacon of hope for families facing similar challenges. What advice do you wish you had known earlier?

A: I wish I had found the School Avoidance Alliance much earlier; we went through a year of feeling lost and awful as parents. My daughter would have suffered a lot less if we'd stumbled upon the group earlier. There is so much that schools are still getting wrong about this, and I hope your book and our advocacy can help remedy the problem!

Q: Do you have any thoughts or experiences you'd like to share about medications that were helpful for your child?

A: Our daughter also has ADHD, which complicates things, but the meds do help with that (Vyvanse and Adderall have been two she's taken; she's currently taking Vyvanse). She has also been on various anxiety/antidepressant meds, including Prozac and Lexapro. She's currently on Wellbutrin. One med that has made a big difference in her mood swings is Abilify, a mood stabilizer, which she has been taking for the past six months. That was a game-changing med, suggested by a second medication provider after our first one had given up on us and said, "There's nothing more that I can recommend."

Q: Do you have any words of hope or encouragement for families who may be struggling right now?

A: Please don't give up. We had to try so many different methods, teachers, programs, meds until we started making progress. And never give up on your child, even though I totally get how extremely difficult this all is. It's not a reflection on you as a parent—your child is suffering, and it would be difficult for anyone to handle. They need you to be the compassionate rock in their life. School is not as important as their overall mental health (though for some kids, doing well in school is part of good mental health—this was our biggest challenge with our daughter, since she was a very good student before all this happened and was so distressed she was missing so much school).

Also, follow your instincts—if you really feel in your gut that something suggested to you would harm your child more than help, take a step back and listen to your gut. Every day, I lived in fear of making things worse—and we did make mistakes, but for the most part, I don't regret following my instincts on what was best for my daughter, even if it made other people annoyed or judgey.

I also recommend seeking therapy for yourself to get you through this—I would not have been able to make it through the past two years without a therapist.

Parent Story 4, by S.Z.

Q: Could you start by sharing some brief information about your child to help other families see how your situation might relate to theirs?

A: My son had trouble transitioning to preschool. He was excited for kindergarten, but the excitement quickly waned. At that point he had all the services due to disability. He was doing so well that in the second grade they said he must not need them and pulled them. As I predicted at the time, this caused a complete unraveling. Within a year he had suicidal ideation with a plan, and he was failing in all subjects at school. It completely altered his relationship with school, and though within two years we had fought hard and won many of his services back, he never was the same. The transition to middle school was probably one of the most painful periods, and the first more traditional signs of school avoidance began to emerge at that point, albeit in minor ways such as refusing to do some assignments. His last high school neuropsych included diagnoses of autism, developmental coordination disorder, generalized anxiety disorder, social anxiety disorder, major depressive disorder, specific learning disorders (multiple), and ADHD. It also indicated some signs of OCD, but just under the diagnostic criteria.

My son's struggles with school had gone on for many years, but they didn't get really bad until he was in ninth grade—his first year of high school—the year after the first COVID shutdown. I should have known where things were headed because even before the COVID shutdown, my son asked if it was possible to take a "gap year" before starting high school. He was tired.

He has always been a kid who thrives when he can move at his own pace and have breaks when he needs them. At that point, I had seen him start and suddenly stop multiple personal projects—learning particular computer games, learning to fly a drone, and so on—only to pick the same projects up six months, a year, or two years later to successfully complete them. He just needs time.

Unfortunately, I had to break the news to him that public schooling doesn't allow kids to go at their own pace or rest when they need to. However, when the shutdown occurred, unlike for my younger child who suffered from the social isolation, my son began to enjoy school a little more again.

It was hard to get him out of bed and up and working for the day, but throughout the shutdown, his eighth-grade special education teacher would call him each morning and do about an hour of work with him on his own. That personal attention free from the demands of constant social interaction worked out well for him. When he started high school, even without the aid of a phone call from a special education teacher, his teachers all commented that he was doing great in virtual schooling. He kept his camera off, but he stayed engaged in classes and readily answered questions or made comments in the chat.

When the shutdown ended, at first it looked like he was going to do okay. Things weren't perfect. He refused to eat or drink at school, for example. But he went into school without too much complaint and had perfect attendance. However, he had a few teachers who were behaving semi-abusively, and he started talking and worrying about it more and more. He is autistic and depends on predictability, but he could not figure out any patterns to help him with these teachers. I requested he be moved to different classes, but it wasn't possible in all cases, so while I continued to work with the school on addressing teacher behaviors, we tried to strategize together about how he could manage in the environments he had to endure.

I could tell his anxiety levels were starting to rise and become unmanageable enough that things were not going to go well. Though he was doing his best to get by, his anxiety about going to school was becoming unmanageable for him. At that point, he and I went and met with the vice principal. The vice principal was surprised to see us because my son hadn't been on his radar at all. I said, "I know he isn't on your radar yet, but I also know his patterns, and his anxiety about school is becoming increasingly difficult for him to manage." I had seen my son spiral, but the school had never seen it. They weren't too worried at that point.

The vice principal at the time was very kind and understanding, however, because he had a daughter who struggled with anxiety also. He told my son not to check his grades in PowerSchool every day, for example, which was a good instruction to give him. At that time, my son was in the habit of looking at his grades multiple times a day, each time spiraling into catastrophic thinking.

But the vice principal also used his experience with his daughter to inform his interactions with my son, even though the needs were a little different. He told my son not to worry about perfect attendance (something he *hadn't* worried about at that point, but that the vice principal's daughter had). He thought perhaps my son was putting too much pressure on himself to show up perfectly and do perfectly in his classes. He said, "The worst thing that happens if you miss some days is that you won't get the perfect attendance award at graduation."

My son depends heavily on rules and statements of boundaries. When the vice principal said that to him, my son took that to mean that the school was unconcerned with attendance. This opened a gate to a new strategy in addressing his anxiety: avoidance. He began to go in later and later each day, reminding me each time that the vice principal said it was okay to miss classes if he needed to. At first he would log in online, but eventually that option became unavailable as the school became more and more focused on getting kids to physically come into the building. Then he would do work from home, even without the option to log in virtually. But he missed enough instructional time that eventually that became quite difficult. At that point, he started missing more whole days.

The more I pushed my son to go, the more he complained of physical symptoms: headaches and stomachaches. These were not new complaints, but he no longer was open to taking some medicine and getting on with his day. Now the only answer when he felt these symptoms was to stay at home. When we hit rock bottom, my son was going to school no more than a few hours a week. It was a self-reinforcing cycle. The more school he missed, the more anxious he became about how far behind he was, and the less likely he was to go the next day. Though I could see this clearly from the outside, my son insisted his anxiety was worse when he went. As he fell further behind, he wasn't just impacted by anxiety, but he began to have a major depressive episode. He started to sleep all day. He barely ate. This was dangerous because he already had ARFID [avoidant/restrictive food intake disorder]. He was over 6 feet tall and just 118 pounds, so every missed meal was a real loss.

He felt hopeless and desperately lonely. He talked a lot about having no friends, about how he couldn't connect with the other kids at school even when he was there. He also would say, "I have no future." He started calling himself "stupid" constantly and talked nonstop about how incompetent he was.

He believed that he did not have the capacity to finish high school. Even after he got a job at sixteen and was doing great with it, he recognized that his older coworkers earning minimum wage were not doing well at all. He noticed that they had to work basically around the clock and were still barely able to survive. He concluded that he was going to have to accept that he was headed for "destitution" and imagined himself eventually becoming an unhoused adult.

Q: What therapy worked and what didn't?

A: In the beginning, nothing worked. He felt too hopeless. I remember the week we basically "got fired" from both his therapist and his psychiatrist. The therapist told us he wasn't engaging at all and that "maybe if he gets on meds, once he is doing a little better, you can bring him back and someone here can get him to engage, but until he starts meds, I don't think we will be able to do anything." But the one person who could prescribe meds—his psychiatrist—also said she had to stop seeing him. "He has been refusing to take meds for half a year, and I am only allowed to see patients I am managing on meds. I've already kept him on my rolls too long."

I felt as though everyone was giving up on my child. I wasn't sure where to turn. Many years prior, very early in my parenting, I had been introduced to the work of Ross Greene. But it had been a really long time, and I had only used the methods as inspiration in some of my parenting over the years. But at this point, the thought that occurred to me is that if my son no longer had a team, I needed to make it really clear to him that he and I were on the same team. I wanted him to know that I was his partner in this and that I wasn't going to give up.

I watched some Ross Greene videos online. I really don't like Ross Greene. But his Collaborative and Proactive Solutions (CPS) method seemed like a good idea for my kid because it would help my kid to know we were in this together and that I wasn't going to abandon him in his hopelessness. I didn't use the method perfectly, and my son didn't respond in a textbook fashion, but I hung in there and made sure to give my kid a really strong message that we were in this together, that I was his partner.

I also knew he couldn't engage the internal work unless something externally shifted. There is little to be gained in doing therapy to live functionally in a dysfunctional system because the system continues to damage us even if we are coping with those harms better. I wanted the system he was living in to be more functional for him. So with the help of extended family who offered to assist us with the financial burden, we hired an educational advocate for him. This was when things began turning around in a more palpable way. When I was able to say to my son, "I have an advocate and she works in an office with an attorney, and we are going to improve things for you," he allowed himself to feel occasional glimmers of hope. The first thing the advocate did was get him an updated neuropsych evaluation, which I think helped him feel like we had some answers and ways to push for what he needed.

To this day, I think I should have pulled my son from school in the second grade the first time things got bad. I think the school system was not designed for a kid like him, and that keeping him in that system was soul-crushing. But I wasn't able to figure out a way to make that workable for us, so instead, I tried to make the best with the system we were in.

Additionally, we found a workable motivator for my son to start trying meds for his depression and anxiety, and he agreed to do so on the condition that we got GeneSight testing for him first so that we might have some help and didn't have to do as much experimentation to figure out what meds would actually help without giving him a bunch of uncomfortable side effects.

At this point, I got my son's primary care doctor involved. He ruled out a number of potential illnesses that could be producing my son's physical symptoms, and he did two other important things: (1) He connected us with a psychiatrist on his own staff who was willing to provide therapeutic services without calling it therapy (just "meds management"), and who was willing to see my son even if there were times he went off meds; and (2) he referred my son to a functional GI specialist who could address his physical symptoms and had a wrap-around care team, which included a nutritionist and GI psychiatrist who could provide comprehensive support.

What ultimately didn't help? Any kind of DBT or CBT back-fired even though both are widely recognized as effective treatments for anxiety. I have since learned that many autistic teens and adults perceive DBT and CBT as manipulative, which can hinder their effectiveness. It would also backfire if therapists and school social workers tried to teach my son coping skills for anxiety before there were changes to his environment. But later on, his openness to learning coping skills increased as his daily experiences began to improve. Sure, he didn't choose to use those coping skills most of the time, but he was open to practicing them with his providers.

What has helped? Believing him. Advocating for him. Always "taking his side" in symbolic ways/thinking about myself as his partner. Bargaining with him to get him on meds (not just for anxiety and depression, but for his GI issues—there was a whole treatment regimen). Having therapists who provided therapeutic support without talking about it as therapy and treating it as "check-ins." Therapeutic conversations focused on his own goals and his own struggles (his primary self-identified struggle is friendship and the desire for intimacy) rather than on parent and school-staff goals to get him into school. Therapeutic conversations that were about practical things, like joining a dating app, rather than things that feel to him more internal, like his thoughts and feelings.

Q: Did your child try any programs or treatments (intensive outpatient, partial program, inpatient) that helped them make progress? If so, what aspects helped your child? Feel free to share the names of treatment programs you recommend.

A: No. My son is really afraid to be seen in his vulnerability. It was clear that if we sought help, even calling for crisis intervention to come help us in our home on a difficult morning when he was in a state of total despair, it would end his trust in us, thus undermining any other work we could do with him. He needed to be in complete control about when he shared and how much he shared, and when he got help, and how much the help impacted his daily life.

Q: Did you make any changes in your home environment, parenting approach, actions, or communication style that helped your child?

A: I have described what did help above. And I will add that one of the absolutely most helpful things the advocate did was document that his attendance issues were related to his disability so that it became the school's responsibility to address it, not ours. If the pressure had remained on us, and we had to live in fear of legal action against us for his absenteeism/"educational neglect," I am certain my son would have been destroyed in the process. Once I stopped worrying that the state would come after us, I was 100 percent a better and more effective parent.

During that time of fear, I did try a strategy that is often recommended but that I now firmly believe is damaging. The approach involved simultaneously teaching coping skills and as those skills improve, to encourage a gradual, parallel exposure to the school environment, while also making home a less comfortable place to be (not allowing electronics use during the day, for example). First, as I mentioned, my son had zero interest in practicing coping skills while being forced into an environment that was deeply traumatic for him—one designed for neurotypicals and staffed with teachers who exhibited abusive behavior. The whole thing backfired: The less comfortable home became, the more hopelessness my son felt, and the more his depression deepened. He was in a very scary place, mentally. He needed home to be a sanctuary.

Q: What accommodations, modifications, or services from your school are helping (or helped) you make progress?

A: What helped was asking him to do work when he was there, but not asking him to make up work from when he wasn't there; minimizing homework and eliminating multi-step projects; allowing him to turn things in as late as he needed (no limits of work acceptance); allowing him to use AI as a tool in his writing process (personalized to his needs); allowing him to use the special ed resource room as often as he wanted to minimize his time in the general setting; helping him nurture close relationships with teachers he liked and trusted (for example, he would go hang out with them during lunch); giving him choices about what he wanted to work on and when; and encouraging teachers to use strategies recommended by the UK's PDA Society (with the exception of declarative language), to encourage better collaboration despite his demand avoidance. He was also exempted from certain graduation requirements, such as gym and art classes, and his math curriculum was completely modified.

Q: Are there any pitfalls or challenges you faced when engaging with your school that you think other families should be aware of?

A: If I could go back in time, and if I knew my family would end up supporting us financially the way they did, I would have hired an educational advocate a long time ago. So much of the damage done to my son in school was cumulative, starting from his earliest years of public education.

Also, I think technical high schools would be awesome for kids like my son if they actually emphasized hands-on learning. However, it is important for parents to know that state curriculum requirements remain, so the hands-on education can only take place if the kids work at double the pace on their academics.

Q: Do you want to share anything about any intervention plan, 504, or IEP for your child? What aspects helped and what was not helpful in them?

A: Even with the advocate, our IEP wasn't great. The school was awful with this stuff. But we had a lot of informal modifications in place that were followed even if not legally required by the IEP.

Q: Do (or did) you utilize an alternative school to help your child get back to learning?

A: No, my son is very much a "the devil you know" vs. "the devil you don't know" person and refused to try other schools. Also, even before all this happened I had looked at Fusion Academy and would absolutely have loved to put him there. I think it would have saved so much of his education. But financially that wasn't a possibility for us, and unfortunately it felt too difficult to get it covered through the IEP process since it isn't categorized as a state-approved therapeutic school.

Q: What advice do you wish you had known earlier?

A: I think it is important not to make assumptions about our kids' futures based on their experiences in school. A lifetime is a long time to learn. My son has now graduated from high school and is finding his way creatively. He is still quite lonely, and the one thing I wish for him is a way to make friends, but now he can make his way through life at his own pace and in his own unique way, and it is awesome to watch it unfold. I have a lot of hope for him. He truly is an amazing kid.

I also think it is so easy to get really scared and focus on consequences and trying to force our kids into compliance. There is a myth that school avoidance comes from lax parenting, or that it is the result of parents not putting limits on their kids, just feeding their anxiety by being responsive to it. But I emphasized limits and avoided being responsive to my kid's anxiety—only to wreck my relationship with my kid at the time when he needed that relationship to be at its strongest. It never changed his behavior. You can't prevent school avoidance by being a strict enough parent, and anxiety that is already present isn't going to go away just because you don't feed it. I think a lot of currently popular therapeutic approaches will eventually be disproven (like the "refrigerator moms" theory of autism from long ago).

To parents I would say: Prioritize your relationship with your kid. Make *that* your first and most important goal. When the trust between you is broken, you won't be able to do them any good anyway, and rebuilding trust is a long, hard road. In the beginning, the school kept pushing me to force my kid into school against his will, even when he was towering over everyone in our family and there was no physical way to bring him in to school. There is so much I did that broke trust between us during that time. All the pushing I did to get him to function—even my belief that he would be fine if he would just go for a little bit—it made him feel unsafe with me. He knew my goal in doing the things he was doing was not his wellness, but compliance with the school's demands. When it got to the point where the only real goal we could have was keeping our kid alive—to ensure he did not end his own life by his next birthday—we knew with heightened clarity that we no longer wanted to be acting as agents of the state in trying to force our kid to comply in his schooling.

I want to be very clear about something: We can address school avoidance on the individual and school levels, but the truth is, it will continue to be an issue until there is massive reform to our educational methods. The environment is harmful. While we were eventually able to get my kid through the system so that he could have some benefit (a diploma that would open up more jobs), for all of his years of pain, his sense of self was sacrificed in the process. His curiosity, wonder, and love of learning; his belief in his worth and dignity was all seriously damaged. It is still going to take him years to heal from this, and the scars will almost certainly never disappear. More than anything, this experience has made me an advocate for educational reform. Our kids are just canaries in coal mines, letting us know that what we are doing is toxic. We need to change what we are doing.

Q: Do you have any thoughts or experiences you'd like to share about medications that were helpful for your child?

A: I know GeneSight testing is not necessarily effective for everyone, but it actually worked well for us, and my son wouldn't have started meds without it.

Parent Story 5, by E.M.

Q: When did school avoidance start, and how did it progress? Was there any diagnosed learning disability or mental health challenge, and was your school cooperative?

A: Our child's struggle with attending school came following what I can only describe as a perfect storm of events that left them feeling challenged: undiagnosed AuDHD [Autism Spectrum Disorder with Attention-Deficit/Hyperactivity Disorder], being fifteen, starting high school in a new state during COVID, and their only sibling going away to college.

In elementary and middle school, they had attended regularly and were actually quite independent and academically successful. However, we did overlook some signs of the AuDHD our child was later diagnosed with (such as differences in interests and communication style relative to peers; expressed discomfort due to sensitivity to clothing, lighting, noises, and change in routine). They never had major problems due to these differences, and we've come to understand that we share these traits as a family, so they were easy to dismiss as quirks.

The challenges of moving to a new state as a high school freshman coincided with hybrid learning due to COVID and masked fall term. This triggered acute homesickness and feeling awkward and lonely in the new environment, until they gave up on meeting new friends and asked to take the option of online learning following the holiday break. This was probably a mistake because they increasingly had anxiety in public spaces and Zoom spaces, even to the point of panic attacks and selective mutism. They also fell into depression, hardly leaving their room for several months. At the time, few mental health professionals had room for new patients, plus our child refused Zoom sessions. At one point we discovered our child missed two weeks of online classes. Luckily, the school allowed the work to be made up. Outside of school, our child would have panic attacks when trying to be in public spaces such as stores or restaurants and would become visibly ill and have to leave those places. We were so grateful that we then got a call that there was a psychiatry fellow starting their training in person, and she welcomed our child as a patient.

Returning to in-person school the next fall, attendance continued to be a struggle despite making progress in therapy and beginning to make friends. Feeling sick, anxious, and panicked were the main complaints.

Q: What therapy worked, and what didn't?

A: Our teen was so anxious going to their first therapy session that they could not speak at all and only nodded as a response. But they liked the doctor on a personal level and returned weekly for three years. The doctor had a no-pressure approach, gradually building connections and trust. It was many months, I believe, until it evolved beyond talk therapy to include CBT, and some exposure therapy around some triggers like eating in front of people and practicing advocating for themself. There was also medication for depression, anxiety, and ADHD. One of the most useful medications in terms of getting over the hurdle of starting a school day was propranolol, taken only on days needed. The doctor described this as a medication sometimes used to help people get over stage fright. There were some medications that did not work well, but within one year we seemed to hit an effective regimen. Our child was very good about taking their medication as prescribed.

Q: Did you make any changes to your home environment, parenting approach, actions, or communication style that helped your child?

A: Yes. Our biggest change was a conscious effort to avoid showing our own anxiety around school and absences, or adding pressure around performance. We focused on reassurance that things will get better gradually, because we trust that they are doing their best. This messaging seemed to change the dynamic to where they truly believed that we, along with the therapist and school, were really on their side ready to give them support.

One small routine that I believe was helpful was asking the night before a school day what they would like for breakfast and then waking them up with delivery of their choice. My theory was that it subtly expresses the general expectation of school, while serving as a subtle reminder that their overall well-being is really important. If they went to school, it was with nourishment. If it was a day they could not make it in, the breakfast still couldn't hurt.

Our approach was completely nonpunitive, which I believe was critical for our sensitive child. Particularly given the period of isolation that kicked this off, we cheered every activity or outing with a friend, whether or not they felt able to attend that day. Our rationale was that it was like exposure therapy and that the more they built positive associations with people from school, the better they would tolerate the school day.

Q: What accommodations, modifications, or services from your school are helping (or helped) you make progress?

A: Our child was at a very highly rated, midsize public school. About six months after we contacted them about the challenges our child was facing and their diagnosis with a letter from the psychiatrist, they did arrange for a psychosocial evaluation so that a 504 could be formally put into place. That process was smooth, but we did have to push for accommodations despite the results, the recommendations of the psychiatrist, and our child's struggles. The factor that seemed to influence the hesitation to provide accommodations was that the teacher evaluations suggested they could not see a problem with a pleasant, quiet student who gets good grades when actually in class. In fairness, each of them saw my child for two periods per week (block schedule) and their student was putting a lot of energy into masking their challenges during those classes. We did ultimately get an accommodation for AirPods with low music to help with focus and reduce stress and sensitivity to other noises. And the school also gave permission to leave class if anxiety peaked, but they rarely used this because they didn't want to gain attention.

Even more than the accommodations, staff interactions tended to impact our child's attendance. Aside from some great teachers, there was a social worker who my child enjoyed meeting with at intervals, informal and friendly. She was also meant as a resource to go to in the event of a panic attack rather than leaving; however, it was rare that the social worker was available at the particular times needed. The office staff and principal also helped through a friendly and supportive approach to late arrivals or early dismissals.

On the flip side, we had a situation where a bullying, self-professed "old-school" teacher directly contributed to an extended period of school avoidance and panic attacks. The teacher objected to 504 accommodations and fought them, objected to my child's they/them pronouns and pushed back against them, and began to intentionally draw attention to these things, even confronting them for an explanation of their diagnosis. We followed up with the administration on the 504 and it was enforced. Then, about a week later, the teacher accessed records that included, albeit double crossed out, our child's completely different former name. The teacher had never known our child as that name, yet when next checking homework, he stopped at their desk and referenced that name as if puzzled ostensibly to get a laugh from students. Thankfully, the kids just looked confused, but my child felt humiliated, targeted, and immediately left school. We received a canned apology letter a week later after copying the principal on a complaint. The teacher said he'd assumed it was a nickname; the way his name is Nathanial but someone might ask why he doesn't go by Nate? Our child missed a full week of school due to that incident and then routinely became ill on the days of that class until finally asking to drop the class in February. Thankfully, the tools and supports we had in place helped get them through that setback with their mental health intact.

But again, overall we felt our child was very well supported at school. Returning for senior year we still had the 504 in place, but there was only a handful of absences all year. Our child had turned the corner and was fully engaged in school, including sports and other extracurriculars, and even said they will miss the school!

Q: If your child is attending online school, is it working? Why do you think it worked or didn't work for your child?

A: Our child had some online classes, but these helped to trigger the anxiety around school. Getting on a Zoom class felt impossible to our child, and they would try to sit out of camera range or would skip them altogether. I am not really sure why this became such a trigger.

Q: What helped you get what you needed from the school to help your child?

A: Persistence. The school was very hesitant to engage around accommodations. The biggest challenge seemed to be the guidance counselor (team lead), who seemed to believe each teacher could decide whether to abide by the 504. Once that was sorted out, we were getting what was needed from the school for the most part (with the notable exception of the algebra teacher).

Q: What advice do you wish you had known earlier?

A: How much it matters to your child that you believe them when they say they are struggling and that you are going to be there advocating for them with the school. It makes all the difference when they see the parents and professionals rallying around them in a time of need. It terrifies me to think of where we would be had we not had a lot of the positive support we were able to find when we did.

Q: Do you have any thoughts or experiences you'd like to share about medications that were helpful for your child?

A: Our child was prescribed medication for ADHD and depression. They also used propranolol as needed for days when getting through the door felt hard but when they thought they could get through the day once there.

Q: Do you have any words of hope or encouragement for families who may be struggling right now?

A: High-masking neurodiversity runs in my family, and our child is not a first-generation school avoidant. A significant number of other people in our family struggled with attendance and turning in assignments in high school due to undiagnosed neurodiversity, yet later went on to earn advanced degrees and have successful professional careers. One who had failed algebra twice went on to get a master's in mathematics and become an actuary at the top of her field. We tease that she chose STEM out of spite. But those examples helped me understand that people's paths and timelines are very often not predictable—that it is okay to prioritize mental health and worry about the rest later.

Parent Story 6, by B.J.

Q: Could you start by sharing some brief information about your child to help other families see how your situation might relate to theirs?

A: She was bullied by her best friends, and this happened around the same time as the COVID pandemic. The transition from grammar school to middle school, combined with moving from a single-town grammar school to a regional middle school, was tough. She also experienced a hormonal shift with her period and was newly diagnosed with ADHD and anxiety.

She is currently in her early teens and in middle school. Her challenges began with health issues such as headaches, stomachaches, and a general sense of not feeling well. She would curl up in a ball, unable to speak, and just cry. She said didn't know why. She was later diagnosed with sleep apnea, ADHD, and migraines. The school fought us every step of the way.

Q: What therapy worked and what didn't?

A: We did some 1:1 virtual counseling once we realized what was happening, but it did not help. We did weekly sessions for two to three months.

We have a psychiatrist who also is a D.O. and have appointments where I do most of the talking. This doctor so understands everything! They use both mainstream medications and natural supplements, which have benefited us in every way.

Q: Did you make any changes to your home environment, parenting approach, actions, or communication style that helped your child?

A: What did not help was the following: grounding her, taking away TV, cell phone, etc. What does help is rewarding her for any step toward school and always encouraging and telling her what a good job she is doing. We make sure she knows we see her trying, making progress, and that we understand and support her. We also don't push her to talk about it a lot. Just listening has been a huge help and leads to more talking on her part.

Q: What accommodations, modifications, or services from your school are helping (or helped) you make progress?

A: We have done home instruction for two years, and we feel this has helped her.

She has been bored at home and seems motivated to go back. She will start attending out-of-district school during the first week of September.

She has a lot of accommodations to begin with, so we will see. School held us back a grade but is allowing her to take 1:1 classes and summer classes to catch up and graduate on time. This is a huge motivation and we are hoping it works!

Q: Are there any pitfalls or challenges you faced when engaging with your school that you think other families should be aware of?

A: Start documenting everything in writing from the very beginning, no matter how long you think the issue may last. Send emails summarizing phone conversations, and keep a notebook with all emails, letters, etc. in chronological order. It's a huge help to know exact dates, who you spoke to, and what was said.

Also, consult with a few advocates as soon as possible when attendance starts to decline. They are a huge support, know the laws, and can hold districts accountable to prevent things from getting worse.

Remember, the districts are not your friends and do not always have your child's best interest in mind. Many districts still do not understand school refusal/avoidance.

Q: Do you want to share any specific information about an intervention plan, 504, or IEP for your child?

A: So far, less work and more time to get the work (and any tests) done has helped. With virtual home instruction, it helped to turn her camera off and keep the microphone on. She also had some instruction at the local library during the first year, so school was not associated with home.

Q: Do you have an alternative school helping your child get to school?

A: She is starting an OOD (out-of-district) school in September, and we're hopeful they can help us achieve this. The school seems to understand the situation and feels they can absolutely accomplish this.

Q: If your child is doing online school, is it working? Why do you think it worked or didn't work for your child?

A: I think it gave her time to relax and time to recognize that we understood and were there for her no matter what. I think it may have been less overwhelming.

Q: What helped you get what you needed from the school to help your child?

A: An advocate. Having a lot of support helped me stay strong and do what I believed was right for my child. Not giving in to the district's pressure and letting them bully me. Researching and learning both the laws of my state and the laws of my district was helpful.

Q: What advice do you wish you had known earlier?

A: I wish I had recognized school refusal/avoidance earlier. I wish I did not take things away and ground her, and wish I was there for her right from the beginning. It breaks my heart we didn't know from the beginning.

We also tested and found things like sleep apnea and ADHD that could be contributing factors. Accommodations for ADHD seem to have been helpful so far, and we are still working to identify the root cause of her sleep apnea—it takes some trial and error. It might be related to an underbite, and she's currently using Invisalign, with plans to wear something afterward that may help.

Q: Do you have any comments or information about medications that helped your child?

A: Around the same time as the avoidance, we noticed hormones seemed to play a role since she had just started her period. She was put on birth control pills to help regulate her hormones, and it has helped.

Q: Do you have any words of hope or encouragement for families who may be struggling right now?

A: With a great deal of patience, encouragement, love, and support for the whole family, I believe we can help our kids. We just want our kids happy and healthy. It doesn't matter if they don't go to an Ivy League school.

Parent Story 7, by J.D.

Q: Could you start by sharing some brief information about your child to help other families see how your situation might relate to theirs?

A: My son struggled with significant separation anxiety from when he was a toddler until age ten or so. He also had generalized anxiety and phobias from age five to nine. He was started on medications for depression and anxiety after expressing suicidal ideation at seven years old. He was hospitalized for ten days when he was eight for significant depression and emotional dysregulation. No medications or talk therapy made any significant difference. We tried many different meds, including ones for ADHD, from age seven until about age eleven. We discontinued medications, and it was after that (and when he went through puberty) that we saw a significant decrease in anxiety/depression and increase in emotional regulation.

Q: What therapy worked and what didn't?

A: He met with several private therapists and counselors in school, but he never really engaged in talk therapy and didn't use any coping skills that we taught him. The only therapy that did work was when my husband and I worked with my son's therapist and learned some DBT skills. This helped us manage our own emotions when dealing with our son.

Q: Did your child try any programs or treatments (intensive outpatient, partial, inpatient) that helped them make progress? If so, what aspects helped your child?

A: My son spent ten days in an inpatient facility when he was eight years old. We had him admitted because his dysregulation reached a point where he was destructive and he said he didn't want to be alive repeatedly. This was in the middle of third grade, which was when the school avoidance ramped up significantly from previous years. School attendance improved somewhat afterward, but it wasn't because of positive therapeutic interventions—it was because he was afraid of being sent back to the hospital. It was basically a scare tactic, which greatly saddens me to think about now.

Q: Did you make any changes to your home environment, parenting approaches, actions, or communication style that helped your child?

A: My son struggled with chronic school avoidance for eight years, from first to eighth grade. I educated myself and my husband on emotional dysregulation (Ross Greene's *The Explosive Child* was particularly insightful). I saw my son in a different light. He was oppositional and defiant because he was truly struggling to simply get through every single day. "Kids do well when they can." Parents do, too.

Some cognitive and educational testing was first conducted when my son was in the hospital in third grade. I educated myself on what this testing measured and what the found deficits implied for his future at school. Then I advocated for additional testing in elementary school and got him an IEP.

Despite all of the school services offered and accommodations given through the IEP from fourth to eighth grade, my son continued to struggle to go to school. I really started to pay close attention to his behaviors, responses to school interventions, and the words he was expressing. He whined and complained about hating school. The day was too long. He didn't care about what he was learning.

It didn't mean anything to him. He didn't understand things. He felt he needed to cheat so he wouldn't appear stupid. He would send me videos about how the school system hasn't really changed in over a hundred years. I started to listen to what he was saying and it started to make sense.

I learned about Dr. Naomi Fisher, who talks about school trauma and how for some kids, many kids, the problem isn't with them as we have all been led to believe. The problem is the traditional school environment. Learning about her and other proponents of unschooling and self-directed learning really solidified my belief that the school environment was the wrong environment for my son. After so many years of trying so many things (including an alternative out-of-district school for fragile kids), the only option we had left was to homeschool. My son didn't want to homeschool. He wanted to be "normal" like his friends and be able to wake up early and go to school and do the work and hang out and be social. We wanted him to experience high school. But with all of the missed school over the years, his refusal to use coping skills, and his reluctance to put forth time and energy to accept help from teachers and staff for his learning disabilities, there's no way he could manage in high school.

Q: Do you want to share anything about any intervention plan, 504, or IEP for your child? What aspects helped and what were not helpful in them?

A: They weren't helpful because my son didn't want to receive any help.

Q: Do you have an alternative school helping your child get to school?

A: We tried an out-of-district placement for seventh grade. Avoidance continued. They couldn't help with getting my son up out of bed, dressed, and out the door.

Q: If you are homeschooling, what is working and what are the challenges?

A: We switched to homeschooling in ninth grade after chronic avoidance for eight years. We are taking more of an unschooling/self-directed approach, which works for him because formal curriculum is meaningless to his life. We are, for the most part, deschooling since my son's school experiences left him traumatized and broken. He learned to hate learning. So the priorities have been healing our broken family relationship (the mom is usually the emotional punching bag and seen as the enemy for forcing the kid to go to school); building my son's self esteem and restoring his self-worth (since he feels like a failure); and promoting socializing.

Q: What helped you get what you needed from the school to help your child?

A: Connecting with other parents of Spec Ed kids and learning from Spec Ed advocacy groups.

Q: Your specific advice, based on your personal experience, could be a beacon of hope for families facing similar challenges. What advice do you wish you had known earlier?

A: Teachers and psychologists and school admins don't know what's best for all children. Not all children respond to traditional behavioral interventions like positive and negative reinforcement. There are numerous alternatives to traditional schooling.

Q: Do you have any thoughts or experiences you'd like to share about medications that were helpful for your child?

A: My son was on a number of different medications for anxiety, depression, and ADHD from age seven to eleven. No medication made any significant difference for him. There weren't any adverse reactions; he just didn't respond to any meds. What seemed to help the most in terms of emotional regulation was time and maturity—going through puberty.

Closing Thoughts

Thank you for investing your time and learning into reading this book. I hope you are walking away with newfound knowledge and guidance to help you move forward advocating for your child.

Through my experiences and discussions with school-avoidance families over the past decade, I have a few final thoughts:

- **Dealing with school avoidance can be scary, draining, and may make you feel as if you are breaking down mentally.** This is not uncommon, but nonetheless, you deserve support, assistance, and compassion. Please do not ignore your mental health. I know you are busy and completely consumed with your day-to-day responsibilities and obligations in addition to doing your best to help your school-avoidant child—*but it is essential that you take care of yourself*. You need more than just standard self-care; yes, it includes getting enough sleep, exercise, eating healthy, talking with friends or family, and maybe getting a mani-pedi. But, most importantly, it means *truly attending to your mental health*.
- **As much as you are able, keep taking steps forward.** You never know when you will find that next therapist, champion, or piece of information to help your child take the next step forward.

- **Helping your child with school avoidance is not a straight line.** It is ups and downs and ups and sideways and ups again (I think you know what I am trying to say).
- **Give yourself grace.** None of this is easy, so please don't beat yourself up. You are a good parent, and you are doing the best you can.
- **Don't get caught up comparing your family to others on social media.** Most people aren't sharing their hardships and struggles or their real lives. You don't need to torture yourself seeing all the posts about amazing kids on their sports teams, going to school functions, and what colleges they are attending. If you don't use FB for support or educational groups or anything else of import, delete it.
- **Kids get back to learning.** We hear this every day from families.

I have seen and spoken to many parents whose children struggled as school-aged kids, either with school avoidance or other challenges. When their child reached their early to mid-twenties, those problems weren't holding them back anymore. They have found their way and are living full, independent, and happy lives.

We are members of a club we would rather not be in, Parents of School-Avoidant Children. Even though our school-avoidance experiences have differences, there are common denominators we all share that bond and unite us.

Please accept my hug, conveying my support and understanding of what you are experiencing. I hope the information and strategies you learned from this book will be helpful to you and your child going forward.

Acknowledgments

For my amazing son, Matthew Evan Demsky, who sacrificed his privacy and allowed me to share his deeply personal and challenging years with school avoidance to help other children and families. My heart is filled with pride and joy for the person you are.

To my husband, Alan Demsky, whom I fell in love with at first sight in the summer of 1985 in a college calculus class for scientists and engineers that we both mistakenly thought was for business majors. We both failed the course, but I won a loving partner who is my rock, providing me with endless encouragement, fun, and laughter and support and excitement about this book.

For my inspiring, compassionate, and hilarious daughter, Jessica Rae Demsky, for your love, smiles, hugs, and stalwart endorsement of my work. Thank you for understanding the times I was absent while writing this book.

I am grateful to my brother, Michael Rosen, for always being there to comfort me in times of doubt, always being the voice of reason, listening to me complain during my months of freaking out while trying to write a book and run a business at the same time, and always ensuring a good time. And for keeping true to Mom's greatest wish.

I sincerely thank my Aunt Ellen Dolgin, Uncle Dr. Stephen Dolgin, and Cousin Joanna Dolgin Kahn for convincing me that I had the knowledge and capability to write this book, when I felt it wasn't possible.

For the following professionals who saved Matt and our family during those scary years of school avoidance. Thank you to Dr. Raul Silva; Special Education Attorney Karen Edler; Lauren Seltzer, LMFT, Jeremy Jordan, and Peter Chorney from the Grove School in Connecticut; and Dennis Fougere and all the staff from Darrow School.

I deeply appreciate my literary agent, Kim Perel of Highline Literary. Thank you for fueling my decision to say yes and write this book. Your expert and friendly guidance eased any stress I felt at every step, and I am truly grateful for your unwavering support. Kim's responsiveness and dedication made an immeasurable difference throughout this journey. There is no doubt that without her expertise, encouragement, and steady presence, I would have struggled to write and promote this book while keeping my sanity intact. Her commitment went far beyond the expected, ensuring that every challenge felt manageable and every milestone achievable. Kim, you are a gift, and I am beyond grateful to have had you by my side.

OMG, this book would have been a mess without the assistance of my developmental editor, the talented Erin Austen Abbot. Thank you for all your suggestions for reorganizing my writing and keeping me somewhat sane during this process.

Thank you, Union Square & Co., for asking me to write this book. I wouldn't have written it without your offer. You made me realize that a book with this information needs to be in the hands of families as soon as possible.

Thank you and appreciation to the editor of this book, Danielle Curtis, for your patience and professionalism in ensuring its quality and timing. You definitely showed grace and restraint shielding me from the stress and challenges you faced working with me, an inexperienced first-time author. A special thank you to executive editor Barbara Berger for her keen editorial instincts and thoughtful articulation, which truly enhanced this work. I also extend my appreciation to project editor Kristin Mandaglio—thank you for your time, effort, and dedication; your contributions have truly made a difference. To cover designer Kaylie Pendleton—I am incredibly grateful for the stunning cover design you created. It beautifully captures the essence of the book, elevating both its marketability and messaging. Thank you to interior designer Christine Heun for the thoughtful layout and visual presentation, which brought clarity and elegance to the book's interior. And to production manager Sandy Noman, your commitment and attention to detail throughout this process were invaluable.

I am forever grateful to the following professionals who agreed to contribute to this project. You are always busy and nonstop with your clients, conferences, and plate full of commitments, not to mention your families and lives. You are a dream team of professionals dedicated to improving lives by spreading awareness and much-needed information on school avoidance. Thank you, Dr. Daniel Villiers, Dr. Rebecca Sachs, Dr. Erica Miller, Dr. Dina Nunziato, Dr. Mona Potter, Dr. Rebecca Etkin, Dr. Tammy Moscrip, Dr. Chris Kearney, Dr. Karen Cassiday, Dr. Scott Hannan, Penny Williams, Willow Williams, and the unnamed special education attorney, for your gift of time and expertise.

Please forgive me for going longer in these acknowledgments, but I must also thank the following people who shared their time, information, and support for my work over these years: Dr. David Heyne, Dr. Anne Marie Albano, Dr. Jonathan Dalton, Dr. Anthony Puliafico, Dr. John Piacentini, Krystina Dawson, Andrew Meltzer, Ivo Pozharliev, Adam Palmer, Linda Geiger, Erica Franceski, Dr. Brian Chu, Karen Edler, Dr. Matthew Murphy, Jonathan Brandt, Ray Renshaw, Dr. Eli Lebowitz, Dr. Naoki Maeda, and Dr. Carolyn Gentle-Genitty.

For the parents and caregivers with children who have or had school avoidance and the families from our parent peer-to-peer support group: Hugs and appreciation for your never-ending determination and perseverance to help your children. Your children are fortunate to have you on their side.

Resources

SCHOOL REFUSAL ASSESSMENT SCALE—REVISED (SRAS-R) FOR PARENTS

Please select the answer that best fits the following questions. For scoring instructions, please see page 256:

1. How often does your child have bad feelings about going to school because he/she is afraid of something related to school (e.g., tests, school bus, teacher, fire alarm)?

0	1	2	3	4	5	6
Almost Never	Seldom	Sometimes	Half the Time	Usually	Almost Always	Always

---

2. How often does your child stay away from school because it is hard for him/her to speak with the other kids at school?

0	1	2	3	4	5	6
Almost Never	Seldom	Sometimes	Half the Time	Usually	Almost Always	Always

---

3. How often does your child feel he/she would rather be with you or your spouse than go to school?

0	1	2	3	4	5	6
Almost Never	Seldom	Sometimes	Half the Time	Usually	Almost Always	Always

---

4. When your child is not in school during the week (Monday to Friday), how often does he/she leave the house and do something fun?

0	1	2	3	4	5	6
Almost Never	Seldom	Sometimes	Half the Time	Usually	Almost Always	Always

5. How often does your child stay away from school because he/she will feel sad or depressed if he/she goes?

0	1	2	3	4	5	6
Almost Never	Seldom	Sometimes	Half the Time	Usually	Almost Always	Always

6. How often does your child stay away from school because he/she feels embarrassed in front of other people at school?

0	1	2	3	4	5	6
Almost Never	Seldom	Sometimes	Half the Time	Usually	Almost Always	Always

7. How often does your child think about you or your spouse or family when in school?

0	1	2	3	4	5	6
Almost Never	Seldom	Sometimes	Half the Time	Usually	Almost Always	Always

8. When your child is not in school during the week (Monday to Friday), how often does he/she talk to or see other people (other than his/her family)?

0	1	2	3	4	5	6
Almost Never	Seldom	Sometimes	Half the Time	Usually	Almost Always	Always

9. How often does your child feel worse at school (e.g., scared, nervous, or sad) compared to how he/she feels at home with friends?

0	1	2	3	4	5	6
Almost Never	Seldom	Sometimes	Half the Time	Usually	Almost Always	Always

10. How often does your child stay away from school because he/she does not have many friends there?

0	1	2	3	4	5	6
Almost Never	Seldom	Sometimes	Half the Time	Usually	Almost Always	Always

11. How much would your child rather be with his/her family than go to school?

0	1	2	3	4	5	6
Almost Never	Seldom	Sometimes	Half the Time	Usually	Almost Always	Always

12. When your child is not in school during the week (Monday to Friday), how much does he/she enjoy doing different things (e.g., being with friends, going places)?

0	**1**	**2**	**3**	**4**	**5**	**6**
Almost Never	Seldom	Sometimes	Half the Time	Usually	Almost Always	Always

13. How often does your child have bad feelings about school (e.g., scared, nervous, or sad) when he/she thinks about school on Saturday and Sunday?

0	**1**	**2**	**3**	**4**	**5**	**6**
Almost Never	Seldom	Sometimes	Half the Time	Usually	Almost Always	Always

14. How often does your child stay away from certain places in school (e.g., hallways, places where certain groups of people are) where he/she would have to talk to someone?

0	**1**	**2**	**3**	**4**	**5**	**6**
Almost Never	Seldom	Sometimes	Half the Time	Usually	Almost Always	Always

15. How much would your child rather be taught by you or your spouse at home than by his/her teacher at school?

0	**1**	**2**	**3**	**4**	**5**	**6**
Almost Never	Seldom	Sometimes	Half the Time	Usually	Almost Always	Always

16. How often does your child refuse to go to school because he/she wants to have fun outside of school?

0	**1**	**2**	**3**	**4**	**5**	**6**
Almost Never	Seldom	Sometimes	Half the Time	Usually	Almost Always	Always

17. If your child had fewer bad feelings (e.g., scared, nervous, sad) about school, would it be easier for him/her to go to school?

0	**1**	**2**	**3**	**4**	**5**	**6**
Almost Never	Seldom	Sometimes	Half the Time	Usually	Almost Always	Always

18. If it were easier for your child to make new friends, would it be easier for him/her to go to school?

0	1	2	3	4	5	6
Almost Never	Seldom	Sometimes	Half the Time	Usually	Almost Always	Always

19. Would it be easier for your child to go to school if you or your spouse went with him/her?

0	1	2	3	4	5	6
Almost Never	Seldom	Sometimes	Half the Time	Usually	Almost Always	Always

20. Would it be easier for your child to go to school if he/she could do more things he/she likes to do after school hours (e.g., being with friends)?

0	1	2	3	4	5	6
Almost Never	Seldom	Sometimes	Half the Time	Usually	Almost Always	Always

21. How much more does your child have bad feelings about school (e.g., scared, nervous, or sad) compared to other kids his/her age?

0	1	2	3	4	5	6
Almost Never	Seldom	Sometimes	Half the Time	Usually	Almost Always	Always

22. How often does your child stay away from people at school compared to other kids his/her age?

0	1	2	3	4	5	6
Almost Never	Seldom	Sometimes	Half the Time	Usually	Almost Always	Always

23. Would your child like to be home with you or your spouse more than other kids his/her age would?

0	1	2	3	4	5	6
Almost Never	Seldom	Sometimes	Half the Time	Usually	Almost Always	Always

24. Would your child rather be doing fun things outside of school more than most kids his/her age?

0	1	2	3	4	5	6
Almost Never	Seldom	Sometimes	Half the Time	Usually	Almost Always	Always

SRAS-R FOR STUDENTS

Please select the answer that best fits the following questions. For scoring instructions, please see page 256:

1. How often do you have bad feelings about going to school because you are afraid of something related to school (for example, tests, school bus, teacher, fire alarm)?

0	1	2	3	4	5	6
Almost Never	Seldom	Sometimes	Half the Time	Usually	Almost Always	Always

---

2. How often do you stay away from school because it is hard to speak with the other kids at school?

0	1	2	3	4	5	6
Almost Never	Seldom	Sometimes	Half the Time	Usually	Almost Always	Always

---

3. How often do you feel you would rather be with your parents than go to school?

0	1	2	3	4	5	6
Almost Never	Seldom	Sometimes	Half the Time	Usually	Almost Always	Always

---

4. When you are not in school during the week (Monday to Friday), how often do you leave the house and do something fun?

0	1	2	3	4	5	6
Almost Never	Seldom	Sometimes	Half the Time	Usually	Almost Always	Always

---

5. How often do you stay away from school because you will feel sad or depressed if you go?

0	1	2	3	4	5	6
Almost Never	Seldom	Sometimes	Half the Time	Usually	Almost Always	Always

---

6. How often do you stay away from school because you feel embarrassed in front of other people at school?

0	1	2	3	4	5	6
Almost Never	Seldom	Sometimes	Half the Time	Usually	Almost Always	Always

---

7. How often do you think about your parents or family when in school?

0	1	2	3	4	5	6
Almost Never	Seldom	Sometimes	Half the Time	Usually	Almost Always	Always

---

8. When you are not in school during the week (Monday to Friday), how often do you talk to or see other people (other than your family)?

0	1	2	3	4	5	6
Almost Never	Seldom	Sometimes	Half the Time	Usually	Almost Always	Always

---

9. How often do you feel worse at school (for example, scared, nervous, or sad) compared to how you feel at home with friends?

0	1	2	3	4	5	6
Almost Never	Seldom	Sometimes	Half the Time	Usually	Almost Always	Always

---

10. How often do you stay away from school because you do not have many friends there?

0	1	2	3	4	5	6
Almost Never	Seldom	Sometimes	Half the Time	Usually	Almost Always	Always

---

11. How much would you rather be with your family than go to school?

0	1	2	3	4	5	6
Almost Never	Seldom	Sometimes	Half the Time	Usually	Almost Always	Always

---

12. When you are not in school during the week (Monday to Friday), how much do you enjoy doing different things (for example, being with friends, going places)?

0	1	2	3	4	5	6
Almost Never	Seldom	Sometimes	Half the Time	Usually	Almost Always	Always

---

13. How often do you have bad feelings about school (for example, scared, nervous, or sad) when you think about school on Saturday and Sunday?

0	1	2	3	4	5	6
Almost Never	Seldom	Sometimes	Half the Time	Usually	Almost Always	Always

14. How often do you stay away from certain places in school (e.g., hallways, places where certain groups of people are) where you would have to talk to someone?

0	1	2	3	4	5	6
Almost Never	Seldom	Sometimes	Half the Time	Usually	Almost Always	Always

15. How much would you rather be taught by your parents at home than by your teacher at school?

0	1	2	3	4	5	6
Almost Never	Seldom	Sometimes	Half the Time	Usually	Almost Always	Always

16. How often do you refuse to go to school because you want to have fun outside of school?

0	1	2	3	4	5	6
Almost Never	Seldom	Sometimes	Half the Time	Usually	Almost Always	Always

17. If you had less bad feelings (for example, scared, nervous, sad) about school, would it be easier for you to go to school?

0	1	2	3	4	5	6
Almost Never	Seldom	Sometimes	Half the Time	Usually	Almost Always	Always

18. If it were easier for you to make new friends, would it be easier for you to go to school?

0	1	2	3	4	5	6
Almost Never	Seldom	Sometimes	Half the Time	Usually	Almost Always	Always

19. Would it be easier for you to go to school if your parents went with you?

0	1	2	3	4	5	6
Almost Never	Seldom	Sometimes	Half the Time	Usually	Almost Always	Always

20. Would it be easier for you to go to school if you could do more things you like to do after school hours (for example, being with friends)?

0	1	2	3	4	5	6
Almost Never	Seldom	Sometimes	Half the Time	Usually	Almost Always	Always

21. How much more do you have bad feelings about school (for example, scared, nervous, or sad) compared to other kids your age?

0	1	2	3	4	5	6
Almost Never	Seldom	Sometimes	Half the Time	Usually	Almost Always	Always

22. How often do you stay away from people at school compared to other kids your age?

0	1	2	3	4	5	6
Almost Never	Seldom	Sometimes	Half the Time	Usually	Almost Always	Always

23. Would you like to be home with your parents more than other kids your age would?

0	1	2	3	4	5	6
Almost Never	Seldom	Sometimes	Half the Time	Usually	Almost Always	Always

24. Would you rather be doing fun things outside of school more than most kids your age?

0	1	2	3	4	5	6
Almost Never	Seldom	Sometimes	Half the Time	Usually	Almost Always	Always

HOW TO SCORE AND INTERPRET THE SCHOOL REFUSAL ASSESSMENT SCALE (SRAS)

Scoring the SRAS is based on a 0–6 point scale. Each question is scored with the following point value:

0	Never	0
1	Seldom	1
2	Sometimes	2
3	Half the Time	3
4	Usually	4
5	Almost Always	5
6	Always	6

Each item in the question set contributes to a different function, which may be contributing to the child's school-refusal behavior. Total scores may be computed by adding the scores of each of the four functions (each column). Then these function scores are each divided by 6 (the number of scores in each set).

The function with the highest mean score is considered the primary cause of the child's school avoidance. The strength of the remaining functions is considered in the development of an appropriate treatment plan. Scores within 0.50 point of one another are considered equivalent. If the parent and child each do their own questionnaire, you add the parent and child scores and divide by 2 to determine the mean function.

In the example below, since the mean score is highest (4.3) in the Function 1 column, this child avoids staying away from objects or situations at school that make the child feel unpleasant physical symptoms or distress.

1. 3	**2.** 3	**3.** 1	**4.** 0
5. 3	**6.** 3	**7.** 0	**8.** 1
9. 6	**10.** 1	**11.** 3	**12.** 2
13. 5	**14.** 5	**15.** 1	**16.** 0
17. 3	**18.** 2	**19.** 0	**20.** 0
21. 5	**22.** 3	**23.** 1	**24.** 1

Total Score =	26	17	6	4
Mean Score =	26/6 = 4.3	17/6 = 2.8	6/6 = 1	4/6 = .66
Relative Ranking =	1			

TERMS USED TO DESCRIBE SCHOOL ATTENDANCE PROBLEMS: A TIMELINE

Terms for What Is Commonly Understood as School Refusal

Terms	Year	Author(s)
A form of truancy associated with neurosis	1932	Broadwin
Psychoneurotic type of truancy; stay-at-home neuroses	1939	Partridge
School phobia	1941	Johnson, Falstein, Szurek, and Svendsen
Refusal to go to school / reluctance to go to school	1945	Klein
Separation anxiety	1956	Estes, Haylett, and Johnson
A variety of separation anxiety	1957	Kanner
School anxiety	1959	Morgan
Mother-phies	1960	Davidson
School refusal	1960[a]	Hersov
Emotional absenteeism	1964	Frick
Inappropriate home-bound school absence	1980	Waller and Eisenberg
Masquerade syndrome as a variant of school phobia	1980	Waller and Eisenberg
School refusal syndrome	1985	Atkinson, Quarrington, and Cyr
Psychological absentee	1985	Reid
Anxiety-based school refusal	1990	Last and Strauss
Internalizing school refusal disorder	1990	Young, Brasic, Kisnadwala, and Leven[a]
Anxious school refusal	1993[b]	Mouren-Simeoni[b]
School refusal behavior	1993[c]	Kearney[c]
Extended school non-attendance	2014	Gregory and Purcell
School reluctant	2015	Jones and Suveg

Note:

"1960[a]" under "School refusal" references footnote a (see below).
"1993[b]" under "Anxious school refusal" references footnote b.
"1993[c]" under "School refusal behavior" references footnote c.

Terms for What Is Commonly Understood as School Withdrawal

Terms	Year	Author(s)
Unwitting, even wilful encouragement of the parents to keep the child from school	1932	Broadwin
Voluntary absence with parental assent	1962	Kahn and Nursten
Voluntary absence with parental assent	1969	Berg, Nichols, and Pritchard
Parent-condoned category	1977	Hersov
School withdrawal; parental complicity	1978	Berg, Butler, Hullin, Smith, and Tyrer
Voluntary withholding by a parent	1980	Galloway
Family-motivated truancy	1981	Amatu
Condoned absence	1985	Galloway
Covert support for non-attendance	1987	Blagg
Parent-motivated school withdrawal	1996	Kearney and Silverman
Parental condoned absence	1997	Berg

Terms for Collections of School Attendance Problems

Terms	Year	Author(s)
Truancy (all types)	1915	Hiatt
Failures of school attendance (all types)	1962	Kahn and Nursten
Persistent absenteeism (all types)	1976	Galloway
School attendance problems (all types)	1980	Rubenstein and Hastings
Persistent unauthorized absence (all types)	1982	Galloway
Pupil absenteeism (all types)	1986	Carroll
School avoidance behavior (all types)	1990	Taylor & Adelman
School refusal behavior (SR+TR)	1993	Kearney
Child-motivated refusal to attend school (SR+TR)	1996	Kearney and Silverman
Truancy (enrolled, no good reason for absence)	2001	Binler and Kirkland
School avoidance (all types)	2002	Berg
School refusal (SR+TR)	2003	Egger, Costello, and Angold
Non-child-motivated absenteeism (all except SR+TR)	2003	Kearney
Chronic non-attendance (all types)	2003	Lauchlan
School attendance difficulties (all types)	2005	Sheppard
Extended school non-attendance (SR+TR)	2007	Pellegrini
Educational neglect (all types)	2011	Larson, Zuel, and Swanson
Voluntary and involuntary absenteeism (all types)	2016	Birioukov

Footnotes (as cited in original table)

[a] Cited in Kearney (2003)

[b] Cited in Martin, Cabrol, Bouvard, Lepine, and Mouren-Simeoni (1999)

[c] The term was previously used by Kearney and Silverman (1990), but not defined

[d] Cited in Galloway (1980)

Reference

D. Heyne et al., "Differentiation Between School Attendance Problems: Why and How?" *Cognitive and Behavioral Practice* 26, vol. 1 (2019): 8–34 https://doi.org/10.1016/j.cbpra.2018.03.006

Courtesy of Dr. David Heyne

Notes

Chapter 1: School Avoidance—What It Is and Why It Happens

2 *School avoidance has been documented since 1932*: D. Heyne et al., "Differentiation Between School Attendance Problems: Why and How?" *Cognitive and Behavioral Practice* 26, no. 1 (2019): 8–34, https://doi.org/10.1016/j.cbpra.2018.03.006.

2 *As this research highlights, the issue has been around in one form or another*: Heyne et al., "Differentiation Between School Attendance Problems: Why and How?"

6 *School refusal occurs among 1 to 7 percent of youth in the general population and 5 to 16 percent of youth seen in clinical settings*: B. R. Maynard et al., "Treatment for School Refusal Among Children and Adolescents: A Systematic Review and Meta-Analysis," *Research on Social Work Practice* 28, no. 1 (2018): 56–67, https://doi.org/10.1177/1049731515598619. | D. Heyne et al., "A Scoping Review of Constructs Measured Following Intervention for School Refusal: Are We Measuring Up?" *Frontiers in Psychology* 11 (August 20, 2020): 1744, https://doi.org/10.3389/fpsyg.2020.01744.

6 *The data we do have for school avoidance comes from global research studies*: "Number of K-12 Students," *IBISWorld*, May 9, 2024, https://www.ibisworld.com/us/bed/number-of-k-12-students/4251/.

8 *Avoidance is generally considered a maladaptive behavioral response to excessive fear and anxiety*: S. G. Hofmann and A. C. Hay, "Rethinking Avoidance: Toward a Balanced Approach to Avoidance in Treating Anxiety Disorders," *Journal of Anxiety Disorders* 55 (2018): 14–21, https://doi.org/10.1016/j.janxdis.2018.03.004.

9 *By avoiding the anxiety triggers, we teach the brain that avoidance is the only path to relief*: M. Tumilty, "It's Not a Rampaging Hippo, It's a Towel: The Anxiety/Avoidance Cycle and How InStride Health Helps to Break It," *Instride Health*, September 19, 2024, https://www.instride.health/blog/the-anxiety-avoidance-cycle/.

10 *The presence of an anxiety disorder as identified in* Diagnostic and Statistical Manual of Mental Disorders, *5th Edition (DSM-5)*: "DSM 5 Anxiety Disorders (A Complete Guide)," *PsychReel*, October 23, 2020, https://psychreel.com/dsm-5-anxiety-disorders/.

11 *Parents must be committed to helping the child achieve total school attendance except for legitimate reasons*: M. K. Sahoo et al., "School Refusal Behavior: A Narrative Review," *Journal of Indian Association for Child and Adolescent Mental Health* 19, no. 4 (2023): 344–354, https://doi.org/10.1177/09731342231220705.

13 *The Four Functions of School Refusal, originally developed*: C. A. Kearney and W. K. Silverman, "Measuring the Function of School Refusal Behavior: The School Refusal Assessment Scale," *Journal of Clinical Child and Adolescent Psychology* 22, no. 1 (1993): 85–96, https://doi.org/10.1207/s15374424jccp2201_9.

16 *Among those with ADHD, "school aversion" is a common reason for absence*: S. Niemi et al., "School Attendance Problems in Adolescent with Attention Deficit Hyperactivity Disorder," *Frontiers in Psychology* 13 (2022): 1017619, https://doi.org/10.3389/fpsyg.2022.1017619.

18 *Children with ODD may have school refusal behaviors*: C. A. Kearney et al., "The Functional Assessment of School Refusal Behavior," *The Behavior Analyst Today* 5, no. 3 (2004): 275–283, https://doi.org/10.1037/h0100040.

20 *Additionally, a lack of classroom structure and organization has been linked to nonattendance*: T. Havik et al., "School Factors Associated with School Refusal- and Truancy-Related Reasons for School Non-Attendance," *Social Psychology of Education: An International Journal* 18, no. 2 (2015): 221–240.

20 *Extracurricular activities, community service, and career or technical education opportunities help keep children engaged and enrolled*: C. A. Kearney et al., "Reconciling Contemporary Approaches to School Attendance and School Absenteeism: Toward Promotion and Nimble Response, Global Policy Review and Implementation, and Future Adaptability (Part 2)," *Frontiers in Psychology* 10 (2019), https://doi.org/10.3389/fpsyg.2019.02605.

21 *Research on school avoidance is shifting away from blaming*: C. A. Kearney et al., "School Attendance and School Absenteeism: A Primer for the Past, Present, and Theory of Change for the Future," *Frontiers in Education* 7 (2022): 1044608, https://doi.org/10.3389/feduc.2022.1044608.

Chapter 2: Effective Therapies—Exploring Treatment Options

24 *That's because the brain and the gastrointestinal (GI) system are intimately connected*: "The Gut-Brain Connection," *Harvard Health Publishing*, July 18, 2023, https://www.health.harvard.edu/diseases-and-conditions/the-gut-brain-connection.

24 *National Alliance on Mental Health provides detailed descriptions to help you make an informed choice*: "Types of Mental Health Professionals," *NAMI: National Alliance on Mental Illness*, April 2020, https://www.nami.org/about-mental-illness/treatments/types-of-mental-health-professionals.

27 *A study on students with generalized anxiety disorder*: L. S. LaFreniere and M. G. Newman, "Exposing Worry's Deceit: Percentage of Untrue Worries in Generalized Anxiety Disorder Treatment," *Behavior Therapy* 51, no. 3 (2020): 413–423, https://doi.org/10.1016/j.beth.2019.07.003.

28 *"In exposure therapy, clients are asked to confront the situations they fear"*: A. M. Albano, "A CBT Approach for School Refusal," Helsinki Conference on Cognitive-Behavioral Therapy, 2018, Helsinki, Finland.

38 *Here are some common reasons children might resist therapy and how parents can address them*: "When Your Child Doesn't Want to Go to Therapy (But Needs To)," Spence Counseling Center, September 1, 2022, https://spencecounselingcenter.com/when-your-child-doesnt-want-to-go-to-therapy-but-needs-to/.

44 *the length of stay is approximately 4.7 days*: M. Arakelyan et al., "Pediatric Mental Health Hospitalizations at Acute Care Hospitals in the US, 2009–2019," *JAMA* 329, no. 12 (2023): 1000–1011, https://doi.org/10.1001/jama.2023.1992.

Chapter 3: Working with Your School—How to Get the Support Your Child Needs

55 *If your child has a diagnosed disability:* "What Is the Child Study Team," National Association of Special Education Teachers, March 24, 2015, https://www.naset.org/publications/parent-teacher-conference-handouts/what-is-the-child-study-team.

56 *Notably, it does not appear in the law itself, only in its implementation*: V. Park et al., "The Evolution of Response-to-Intervention," in *The Palgrave Handbook of Educational Leadership and Management* (Palgrave Macmillan, 2021), https://ccog.calstate.edu/sites/default/files/2023-07/Park2021_ReferenceWorkEntry_TheEvolutionOfResponse-to-Inte.pdf.

56 *According to the MTSS Center*: S. Durrance, "Implementing MTSS in Secondary Schools: Challenges and Strategies," *Comprehensive Center Network*, January 2023, https://region6cc.uncg.edu/wp-content/uploads/2022/06/ImplementingMTSSinSecondarySchools_2022_RC6_003.pdf.

59 *The following legislation, part of the Texas Education Code Sec. 26.001 (2019)*: "Education Code, Title 2. Public Education, Subtitle E. Students and Parents, Chapter 26. Parental Rights and Responsibilities," https://statutes.capitol.texas.gov/docs/ed/htm/ed.26.htm.

60 *"Parents have the right to request an evaluation"*: S. Bruce, "A Parent's Guide to Response to Intervention (RTI)," *Wrightslaw Special Education Law and Advocacy*, April 20, 2015, https://www.wrightslaw.com/info/rti.parent.guide.htm.

Chapter 4: Educational Rights—Navigating Laws and Protections

65 *Child Find is a federal law*: "Sec. 300.111 Child Find," *Individuals with Disabilities Education Act*, May 3, 2017, https://sites.ed.gov/idea/regs/b/b/300.111.

65 *it would be inconsistent with the IDEA evaluation requirements for a school to reject a referral*: P. Schwinn, "Responsibilities and Timelines Regarding Parent Requests for Special Education Evaluations Under the Individuals with Disabilities Education Act (IDEA), TEC, and TAC," *Texas Education Agency*, February 26, 2018.

68 *The following is a modified sample letter from Ohio Disability Rights Law and Policy Center, Inc.*: "Requesting an Initial Evaluation to Determine if Your Child Is Eligible for Special Education Services," Disability Rights Ohio, https://www.disabilityrightsohio.org/letter-writing-requesting-initial-eval. | "Communicating with Your Child's School Through Letter Writing," Disability Rights Ohio, https://www.disabilityrightsohio.org/communicating-your-childs-school-letter-writing#samples.

74 *a medical diagnosis is* not *required to qualify under Section 504*: "Questions and Answers on the ADA Amendments Act of 2008 for Students with Disabilities Attending Public Elementary and Secondary Schools," US Department of Education, January 14, 2025, https://www.ed.gov/laws-and-policy/individuals-disabilities/section-504/questions-and-answers-on-the-ada-amendments-act-of-2008-for-students-with-disabilities.

74 *the OCR link, "Frequently Asked Questions About Section 504 and the Education of Children with Disabilities," provides helpful clarification and answers*: "Frequently Asked Questions: Section 504 Free Appropriate Public Education (FAPE)," U.S. Department of Education, January 13, 2025, https://www.ed.gov/laws-and-policy/civil-rights-laws/disability-discrimination/frequently-asked-questions-section-504-fape.

75 *If your child qualifies for an IEP*: "Parental Concerns," Disability Law Center of Virginia, December 19, 2014, https://www.dlcv.org/special-ed/iep/parental-concerns.

80 *Executive functioning (EF) skills training*: "Executive Functioning Skills," The Pathway 2 Success, November 20, 2024, https://www.thepathway2success.com/executive-functioning-skills.

81 *Social skills training*: M. Vallejo, "A Guide to Building Strong Social Skills for Teens," *Mental Health Center Kids*, December 22, 2023, https://mentalhealthcenterkids.com/blogs/articles/social-skills-for-teens.

82 *Any other factors or challenges that parents are aware of*: "Parental Concerns," Disability Law Center of Virginia (dLCV), https://www.dlcv.org/wp-content/uploads/2015/06/SE-How-to-Address-Parental-Concerns-6-2015.pdf.

86 *Get Your State's Parent's Guide*: "Get Your State's Guide to Parental Rights in Special Education," School Avoidance Alliance, April 1, 2022, https://schoolavoidance.org/get-your-states-guide-to-special-education/.

Chapter 5: Legal Insights—Pressing Questions Answered by a Special Education Attorney

93 *Refer to the Questions and Answers on the ADA Amendments Act of 2008 for clarification*: "Questions and Answers on the ADA Amendments Act of 2008 for Students with Disabilities Attending Public Elementary and Secondary Schools," U.S. Department of Education, January 10, 2020, https://www.ed.gov/laws-and-policy/individuals-disabilities/section-504/questions-and-answers-on-the-ada-amendments-act-of-2008-for-students-with-disabilities.

96 *"supports parents in getting their children the special education resources they need"*: "Guidelines for Choosing an Advocate," Council of Parent Attorneys and Advocates, https://www.copaa.org/page/GuidelinesAdv.

Chapter 10: The Dreaded T-Word—Truancy

163 *"A complicating feature of the school refusal/truancy distinction"*: J. G. Elliott, "Practitioner Review: School Refusal: Issues of Conceptualisation, Assessment, and Treatment," *The Journal of Child Psychology and Psychiatry and Allied Disciplines* 40, no. 7 (1999): 1001–1012, https://doi.org/10.1111/1469-7610.00519.

168 *"Parents, guardians, or students have multiple chances to show evidence or explain"*: T. C. Johnson, "Unexcused: Do PA Schools Have to Send Kids to Court for Truancy? 4 Debunked Myths," *PublicSource*, October 28, 2021, https://www.publicsource.org/pa-schools-truancy-court-unexcused-absences-myths/. | D. Fowler et al., "Class, Not Court: Reconsidering Texas' Criminalization of Truancy," *Texas Appleseed*, March 2015, https://www.texasappleseed.org/sites/default/files/2023-05/truancyreport-all-final-singlepages.pdf.

171 *"The current, court-centered approach to addressing truancy is not working"*: Fowler et al., "Class, Not Court: Reconsidering Texas' Criminalization of Truancy."

172 *"Research indicates that overly punitive responses to truancy"*: M. McInerney, "Effective Approaches to Increasing Attendance," *Education Law Center*, June 9, 2015, www.elc-pa.org/wp-content/uploads/2015/06/ELC-Testimony-For-Legislative-Hearing-on-Truancy-June-9-2015.pdf.

Chapter 12: Alternative School Options—Exploring New Educational Paths for Success

187 *Learning Lab provides the following criteria to determine if online schooling fits a child*: B. Powers, "Is Online Schooling a Good Fit for Your Child?" *Learning Lab*, October 12, 2016, https://mylearnlab.com/articles/is-online-schooling-a-good-fit-for-your-child.

189 *Adults, sometimes (but not always) parents, typically offer support, assistance, and guidance when needed*: T. Ingram, "The Case for Unschooling," *Vox*, July 20, 2020, https://www.vox.com/first-person/2020/7/17/21328316/covid-19-coronavirus-unschooling-homeschooling.

189 *Unschooling, emphasizing how natural curiosity can lead to effective learning*: P. Gray and G. Riley, "The Challenges and Benefits of Unschooling, According to 232 Families Who Have Chosen That Route," *Journal of Unschooling and Alternative Learning* 7 (December 2013), https://www.researchgate.net/publication/305720522_The_Challenges_and_Benefits_of_Unschooling_According_to_232_Families_Who_Have_Chosen_that_Route.

Index

About the Experts

Dr. Rebecca Etkin is a licensed clinical psychologist and postdoctoral associate at the Yale Child Study Center Anxiety and Mood Disorders Program, where she studies and treats anxiety disorders and related difficulties in children and adolescents. She is a leading SPACE (Supportive Parenting for Anxious Childhood Emotions) clinician, trainer, and supervisor. She has worked with over a hundred families using the SPACE approach.

Dr. Christopher Kearney is a highly respected clinical child psychologist, distinguished professor, and chair in the Department of Psychology at the University of Nevada, Las Vegas (UNLV). He is the creator of the Four Functions of School Refusal and the School Refusal Assessment Scale (SRAS). He also serves as the director of the UNLV Child School Refusal and Anxiety Disorders Clinic. Dr. Kearney's expertise focuses on problematic absenteeism and school refusal behavior in young people. He is widely published in peer-reviewed journals. His books include *Helping School Refusing Children and Their Parents* and *Getting Your Child to Say "Yes" to School: A Guide for Parents of Youth with School Refusal Behavior.*

Dr. Erica Miller is the founder and director of Connected Minds NYC. She is a licensed clinical psychologist in New York and New Jersey, specializing in neuropsychological assessments and evidence-based treatments. She co-founded Successful School Transitions and is an adjunct associate professor at Teachers College, Columbia University.

Dr. Tammy Moscrip is a licensed clinical social worker, the executive director, and chief administrator at the Spire School. She holds a doctorate in psychology and specializes in working with children and families. The Spire School is a Connecticut state-approved special education program and an independent, therapeutic day school for intellectually capable students in grades 8–12 who are struggling academically and emotionally.

Dr. Dina Nunziato is the chief clinical officer of Anxiety Institute in Greenwich, Connecticut. The Anxiety Institute provides intensive outpatient treatment programs and customizable outpatient services for children, adolescents, and young adults with anxiety disorders, OCD, and school avoidance. Dr. Nunziato has helped young adults in anxiety-related clinical and educational settings for over twenty years. She specializes in cognitive behavioral treatment of anxiety and related disorders. Her research and publications include evidence-based mindfulness techniques for anxiety management, academic success, and emotional well-being.

Dr. Mona Potter is a board-certified child and adolescent psychiatrist and the chief medical officer and co-founder of InStride Health, providers of specialty outpatient care for pediatric anxiety, school avoidance, and OCD. As the medical director of McLean Hospital's Child and Adolescent Outpatient Services, she co-developed several programs, including the McLean Anxiety Mastery Program (MAMP) and the McLean School Consultation Service.

Dr. Rebecca Sachs, ABPP, is a clinical psychologist, the founder of CBT Spectrum, and the co-director of Successful School Transitions, a program specializing in school refusal. She is an expert in top-recommended treatments for anxiety, autism, and OCD and is board-certified in behavioral and cognitive psychology. Additionally, she is a mother to an energetic six-year-old and stepmother to a fifteen-year-old.

Dr. Daniel P. Villiers has a PhD in Counseling Psychology, an MEd in School and Applied Child Psychology, and an MA in Cognitive Science. His personal struggle with severe anxiety during high school sparked a deep commitment to developing innovative methods and programs to address the emerging epidemic of youth anxiety in the early 2000s. This dedication led him to co-found Mountain Valley Treatment Center in 2011 and the Anxiety Institute in 2016, both of which have become industry leaders in the residential and outpatient treatment of anxiety disorders, respectively. Over his 21-year career as a scholar-practitioner, Dr. Villiers has developed subspecialties in family-based exposure therapy for pervasive school avoidance and refusal, exposure/response prevention (E/RP) for treating OCD in both neurodiverse and neurotypical teens, and exploring the roles of perfectionism, avoidance, and self-sabotage in anxiety and mood disorders.

Penny Williams is a parenting coach, speaker, and author who works with neurodiverse families. She helps parents navigate the challenges of raising neurodivergent kids using neuroscience-backed insights and strategies. She is the author of four award-winning books on ADHD, including *Boy Without Instructions,* and hosts the *Beautifully Complex* podcast. She is also the co-creator of the Survival to Success Accelerator™, a parent training program.

Willow Williams is a twenty-one-year-old high school graduate and advocate who has autism and who has experienced school avoidance. She is currently exploring career opportunities in various fields, including music, puppeteering, voice acting, nursing, elder care, and construction work. She lives in Asheville, North Carolina, with her parents and two dogs.

About the Author

Jayne Demsky is the founder of the School Avoidance Alliance, where she has dedicated over a decade to empowering families and educational institutions in addressing the complexities of school avoidance.

In 2014, motivated by personal experience and the urgent need for resources, Jayne established the School Avoidance Alliance. The organization was born from the challenges her son faced with chronic school avoidance, filling a critical gap in support, education, and advocacy.

Today, the School Avoidance Alliance is the leading resource for school avoidance professional development across the United States. Their flagship courses—"Everything You Need to Know to Get Your Students Back to School" for educators and the "School Avoidance Master Class for Parents"—have transformed the approach of countless school districts, enhancing their capacity to improve student engagement and success.

Under Jayne's leadership, the Alliance's contributions have garnered national attention, with features in prominent publications and media outlets such as *USA Today*, *Education Week*, *The Washington Post*, EdSurge, *ADDitude Magazine*, Attendance Works, Fox News, *Good Morning Arizona*, and CBS News.